Gathering the
Wayward Heart

Live Life
Forgiven!

Tracey Glenn

Gathering the *Wayward Heart*

Lessons on Faith, Trust, and Surrendering Our Best-laid Plans

Tracey Glenn

ISBN 13: 978-1-64645-265-1(Paperback)
978-1-64645-266-8 (ePub)
978-1-64645-267-5 (Mobi)

Library of Congress Catalog Card Number: 2021913398

Dedication

To my wonderful husband, Link,
my daughter, Taylor,
and her husband, Wyatt,
my daughter, Kaylee, and son, Collin,
and my grandkids,
Kail, Kadence, Karson, and Kole.
You are the lights in my life
and precious gifts from God.

Contents

Acknowledgments

First, I would like to thank the Lord. It was God who instilled in me a desire to write and provided the inspiration and talent. I have survived the trials of life outlined in this book by His hand, and I am grateful for the blessings that have come out of them.

I would like to thank my husband, Link Glenn, who lived through the writing of this devotional. He listened to me prattle on as I attempted to navigate some emotional waters. He is the best husband any woman could ask for and has been by my side in the trials of life. We have grown stronger together through all of it.

I want to thank my daughter, Taylor Klump, who is not only a daughter but a best friend. She has helped me through this process and has been a great support. I am so thankful for her.

I want to thank my sisters Gwen White, Dawn Donnel, Chris Cook, and Laura McDonald. They listened to me, gave me feedback on my lead magnets, read some chapters, and encouraged me through the entire process. I am truly blessed to have four sisters who are also friends. God gave us awesome parents, Jane and Leo Cook, who taught us to keep the drama low and the love high.

I want to thank Carmen Farr for being such a great support to our family and friend to my mom. After we lost Mom, Carmen wrapped her love around us girls and claimed us as her own. Carmen and her husband, Skip, are wonderful people, and their love for the Lord is inspirational.

A huge thank you to Jennifer Edwards, who is the best writing coach and editor I could have hoped for. God matched us up, and I am very appreciative of the help, encouragement, and insight she gave through this entire process.

Thank you to all the ladies at Redemption Press, especially Andrea Tomassi, who encouraged me to write my story, Athena Dean Holtz, who gave me words of wisdom and support and Carol Terzlaff who gave me feedback and support.

To my friend Celia Bernal, who listened to me talk nonstop and gave me encouragement as I traveled the path of self-doubt.

Thank you to my entire launch team.

Introduction

*"For I know the plans I have for you," says the Lord.
"They are plans for good and not for disaster, to give
you a future and a hope."*
Jeremiah 29:11 NLT

Throughout our lifetime, there are events that define us, snapshots in time that mold us into who we are now. These are the pivotal points that often determine our final destination on the road of life. They shape the perceptions we have of ourselves and the person we've become. Usually, we remember them because they correlate with a tragedy or life-altering event. Things said or done to us that impact our thoughts, who we are, and what we believe about ourselves and the world in general. Sometimes these pivotal points place stains on our souls that only God can sponge away.

We enter this earth as empty vessels, and as we travel the path of life, we are filled with things that shape our perspective in life. It is as if we are each handed a pair of glasses that get scratched and cracked on our journey. It is up to us to change our lenses, but if we don't know how to do that, we get accustomed to the view and continue down the same path. We are changed as we go along, influenced first by our parents, then our friends, our choices, and experiences. All create the final version of ourselves that can seem unchangeable. Parental and environmental influence can be good or bad, depending on our parents' character and where we are raised. But our ultimate "destiny" on earth doesn't have to be the final product of our parents or our environment. We do have a say in the matter. We can alter our destiny by modifying our perspective, which we can do by changing the lenses in our glasses. When we evaluate our life based on God's plan, His purpose for us can be vastly different from our worldly ambition.

Children are planners and dreamers, and before the stains of life taint their perspective, nothing is unattainable to a child. As children, we all have future aspirations and an idyllic vision of our final destiny. I was a dreamer with high expectations for my life. When asked what I wanted to be when I grew up, my response always included, "I want people to know I was on this earth; I want to leave a mark." I grew up on a large cattle ranch in Arizona, and our closest neighbor lived in a house several miles down the one road that went to town. I had no neighborhood kids to play with, so I had to entertain myself. I am the youngest of five girls, and the sister closest to me in age is three years older. However, she usually had other things to do, so I typically played by myself.

For a brief period, I aspired to be an actress, and I would go about my day talking to myself, playing some imaginary role in a film. I wrote the screenplay as I acted it out. I envisioned the day when I would be a famous Hollywood actress, beautiful, perfect, and rich. In my mind, I would be instantly discovered and an overnight success. I avoided getting weighed down in the pesky details like the hard work and perseverance, because those eventually doused my passion. Plus, I have always been socially awkward, so acting and stardom was never a very realistic dream for me. I did not know the dedication and fortitude it would take to become "successful" in any part of life.

Some people, however, are driven to succeed, and they follow their dreams with laser focus. With hard work and determination, they beat the odds and flourish. Others, such as myself, are not as resolved and focused on the future. We have big dreams but not enough courage or stamina to stay in the fight. People like us tend to stumble through life, changing direction as the wind blows, and our destination is elusive and a bit abstract.

After I grew out of the movie star years, I became somewhat more grounded and decided to pursue a career in marine biology. I could picture myself loading my pickup and heading out to California; of course, in my vision, I had a nice pickup and a house on the beach—it was a dream after all. I held on to that aspiration through my first year of college. But then I experienced something tragic that changed my entire outlook in life and altered my course.

As a college student, I had a strong desire to please others and needed affirmation from others to bolster my value and worth. I was my own worst enemy and often ended up putting myself in situations that were not only risky but portrayed me as something I was not. One night, I placed myself in a situation that led to date rape, which propelled me head first down a path of abuse from other young men. That fateful night, I paid a price for my reckless behavior, and I plummeted to the bottom of a pit I had dug for myself. I swept humiliation under the rug and kept many secrets to myself. Shattered, I searched for my value and true identity, grabbing for worldly things that I believed would make me whole, but they just left me empty and continuously seeking.

But God knew better, and He reached down and pulled me from the muck and mire I was engulfed in. He set me on a new path, freeing me from my pit. My true Prince had finally arrived, yet the adventure was just beginning. From my first encounter with the Lord, He has faithfully walked with me through all of my trials, down the winding roads of near-death experiences and family hardship we never saw coming. I've come across several people, who I believe were angels, sent to protect and watch over me. I had to overcome my idol worship, walk through the trials of raising a child with special needs, and live apart from a husband who worked far from home much of the time. Through it all, God's overwhelming care and provision for me has been simply breathtaking. He has helped me overcome pain, often self-inflicted, and He has perfected me through fire, refining my actions and reactions to this broken world. And now through this book, He has redeemed me by allowing me to share my lessons and stories to help other women in their struggles and pain.

I believe that God has given me this life and message to encourage others and give them hope. My hope is for this book—this message—to reach the nonbeliever that she may come to know God. May the young believer grow in knowledge and faith. May everyone who reads my words come to understand that God's plan is perfect, and He has given each of us a hope and future that is better than anything we could ever desire or imagine (Ephesians 3:20).

Do you know you are fearfully and wonderfully made, and God knows everything about you? He knew you in your mother's womb (Psalm 139:13–14), and He determines the steps you will take in life up to your last day on this earth (Proverbs 16:9). God has made a way and a plan for you because He has a deep love for His beloved. God will meet you where you are because no matter the place, be it on the highest of mountains or in the deepest of valleys, He is with you. He wants to walk with you. Do you see Him? He stands with an outreached hand, and all you need to do is grab it. We each walk our own path and face unique trials in life. However, our perspective determines our perception and our reaction to life in general.

Introduction

Take it from me when I tell you that having a personal relationship with the Lord will change your life, because when your foundation is firm, your hope and faith is solid, and your path forward is clearer. When trouble comes you may falter, but you will never fall. He won't let you.

I come from a place of extreme imperfection, but God is the perfect Potter, and He continually works to make each of us a masterpiece. Each chapter begins with a trial I endured, followed by my "Afterthought," my retrospective view of each event. Hindsight is usually 20/20 if we allow ourselves to reflect back with honesty. We can see where God was working, and that we were never alone. Since I was raised on a ranch, I developed a "Ranch Talk" section to correlate my life growing up and ranch experiences with God's lessons. The "Faith Lesson" is the overall truth that I feel God revealed to me through the hardship, followed by a prayer that I hope you will pray over your life. Finally, I encourage you to work through the "Study" section, because studying God's Word will help you grow in your knowledge of God and Scripture and will ultimately heal your heart.

I am excited you have decided to take this journey with me. My prayer is that you will see how God can carry you through all difficulty. I am here to testify that Jesus really does leave the ninety-nine to gather one wretched sinner like me (Matthew 18:12; Luke 15:4). He gathered my wayward heart into His arms and branded me as His own. He refined me through fire so I could bloom from the ashes.

Shattered Faith

*Now the serpent was more crafty than any other beast
of the field that the Lord God had made.*
Genesis 3:1 ESV

"The kind flatterer was gone, replaced by the person looking at me with disdain and contempt. I was a piece of trash in his eyes now, the snake in him revealed, and in his mind, it was time to throw me out. I had placed my trust in him, and he crushed my spirit. I felt rejected and alone, my faith shattered."

Scars of the Past

I am thankful God has given each of us free will, meaning we each have a choice where to place our hope and faith. The source of our hope and faith can be a good thing but also a bad thing—people, money, jobs, material possessions, relationships—all are false idols. Idols can do nothing to change our eternal destiny or help us become our final and best version of ourselves. When we put faith in worldly things and not God, whatever it is will eventually end up shattered or it will shatter us. The people and things of this earth will never make us whole, because only God can do that.

In 2 Peter 3:18, we are told to grow in both grace and knowledge through God's Word, meaning we need to become mature in spirit. When we learn what the Bible says about God, ourselves, and others, we develop our spirit. Our faith grows as we come to know the only One who can give us hope and affect lasting change in us. Everyone who reaches adulthood matures in the body, but not all mature in the spirit. The choice to grow is ours.

I came to know the Lord when I was in my early teens. I went with one of my sisters to California, and I prayed for salvation on that trip. I know I received God's saving grace at that moment, but I was far from having a personal relationship with Him. I was still putting my faith in people and things, not God. It took many years of growing before I even began the quest for spiritual maturity. I lived my life based on my own earthly desires, so I continued to live in sin.

My parents were wonderful, loving role models in my life, and I had a great childhood. I grew up on a ranch, and even though we were not wealthy, we had what we needed. Weight was a big issue for my grandparents. My maternal grandmother, Grandma Nelson, was a very petite woman. I can still picture her. She was always impeccably dressed and looked prim and proper. However, I was a chunky kid and a tomboy and never put much thought into my appearance. We would visit my grandparents several times a year, and my paternal grandmother, Grandma Smith, lived about a block from Grandma Nelson. I could walk out the back door of Grandma Smith's house, go down the alley a few houses, and Grandma and Grandpa Nelson's home was just across the street.

I remember when visitors came to the Nelsons, and as I stood looking at two strangers, Grandma Nelson proceeded to introduce me as "the fat one in the family." I can remember it so clearly because those words devastated me. Something that was most likely trivial to her had a profound and long-lasting impact on me. I was humiliated, and that's when I began to see myself as fat and started obsessing about my weight. It was one of those pivotal moments that changed my perception of myself. It put a scratch on the lenses of the glasses I looked through. That experience gave me the false belief that my value was associated with my weight, and thus began the continuous need to be affirmed by others.

There is a common saying, "Words will never hurt me." Well, that is just not accurate at all. I do not think that my grandma wanted this statement to define me. I think she believed she was helping. I hope after she said that, she regretted it, but I do not think she realized the impact those words had on my spirit. Words can have an extreme impact on people, especially children, because they take them to heart. Statistics show that 30,000 American children die every year, and half of those deaths are due to verbal abuse. A child taking their own life because of something said to them is tragic. Words absolutely have an impact.[1]

I started dating boys on the college rodeo team at the end of my senior year in high school and continued through college. I did not maintain long relationships with any of them because I continued to be unwilling to cross that line, which is what they typically sought. Most of these boys were heavy into alcohol and drugs, and they threw a lot of parties. I would usually show up with the guy I was dating at the time and was often the only girl there. I drank alcohol, but drugs never interested me, so I stayed away from them, and no one used them in front of me.

Being the lone girl at the party, I received a lot of attention, which I craved because it was a form of validation for me. It made me feel worthy, wanted, and accepted. I needed to know that I was good enough, skinny enough, and pretty enough. I was by no means the girl who grew up in church and never did anything questionable. I wore miniskirts and half shirts, and I flirted more than I should have. Alcohol emboldened me, and I placed myself in dangerous situations many times. I was, in every sense of the word, a tease.

Many times I would end up behind closed doors in a room with a guy. I would talk incessantly for hours, and we made out, but I never allowed any of them to cross that line. I never thought anything about this, since I knew nothing happened—my conscience was clear. For some reason, though, I never stopped to consider what others thought. I guess I just assumed my friends knew nothing had happened, but how could they? I was building my bad reputation through my own naivety. I had marked myself, and I could not blame anyone else for thinking I was a harlot.

The mark hung on me like a scarlet letter, and even though everyone around me thought I was sexually active, I was not. People talk in small towns, and they believed the worst because that is how I portrayed myself. The girl I showed the world was not an accurate picture of who I truly was. As crazy as it sounds, I was looking for love, and I sincerely believed that one of those boys would be the person I married. At age nineteen, I was still a virgin, and I had no intention of that changing before marriage. I was seeking something vital to me—love and a husband.

I met him in one of my classes. He was not someone I was immediately attracted to, not someone I would have typically dated. He sat behind me and would strike up a conversation every time we had class. He was funny, and at first I had no interest, but he was endearing and a real charmer. He was not like the other rodeo cowboys, whose idea of taking a girl out to dinner was down to the local convenience store; he was different. When he finally asked me out, I said yes.

We hung around together often. He lived off campus, so I did not see him every day. But I wanted to be around him all the time. I lived on campus, so my parents were unaware of anything I was doing when I was away at school. When he asked me to go with him to a rodeo he was entered in and spend the weekend with him, I did not think anything of it. I didn't feel in danger—I completely trusted him.

I left the campus with him on a Friday, and we stayed the night in his house. I slept on the couch. The next two days, we drove to the rodeo, he competed, and we returned each evening to his house. I slept on the couch all three nights. Monday, I rode with him back to the college. I was in heaven and falling in love with this guy. I spent so much time with him that my college roommate was already talking about the wedding! I was in love.

The Urban Dictionary defines "love" thirty-six ways. The number-one definition is, "Love is giving someone the power to destroy you, and trusting them not to."[2]

A far less cynical view of love is the love Jacob had for Rachel—the love story we find in Genesis 29. Jacob loved Rachel so much he was willing to work for seven years for her father on a promise that she would be given to him in marriage. The Bible says that the love Jacob had for Rachel was so great that the seven years seemed like only a few days to him. However, when it came time for Jacob to take Rachel in marriage, her father pulled a fast one and slipped his oldest daughter Leah in there. Undeterred, Jacob was willing to work another seven years for Rachel. That is some deep love—the love a girl only dreams of. That is the love I was sure I had found.

With May quickly approaching and the spring semester coming to an end, I was feeling somewhat depressed. I would go from seeing him several days every week to not getting to see him at all. The dreaded day came when I packed up my dorm room, said my good-byes to friends and my love, and moved back home for the summer. Back to the ranch, the middle of nowhere, where our closest neighbor was several miles down the dirt road.

I spoke to him on the phone often, and as the Fourth of July approached, I received an invitation from him. He wanted me to spend the weekend with him. Since I had already stayed with him once, I was not concerned, and I was excited to get to spend time with him. I went with complete trust.

I drove to a town an hour-and-a-half away, then rode with him and one of his friends to his house. We spent the day looking through the vendor booths, and since he knew everyone, there was a lot of stopping to visit. When evening came, we went back to his place and got ready for the dance. He had been his typical self all day, but about halfway through the night, he was ready to go back to his house. As we walked the short distance home in the dark, I felt like I was walking with a stranger. His mood had changed. He was no longer lighthearted and happy. We entered the house, and when he locked the door behind him, I could feel the tension build. He did not typically lock the door, not even when we left for the day.

He let me know right away that the couch was not an option, but then someone knocked on the door and I sighed with relief. The friend needed a place to sleep, and so I thought, *He will stop if someone is here.* But when he closed the bedroom door, I realized he had not changed his mind. "I don't want to do this," I told him, but he ignored my plea. It was something he would not accept. I did not call out for help. I was afraid and ashamed—I should have cried out. But even if I had, would the friend have helped me? I will never have an answer to that question. I believe it would have been to no avail.

I had placed myself in this position once again, and what happened was out of my control. I wish I could go back in time and change my decision to spend the weekend with him. I wish I could save that stupid girl from her destructive choices. The remainder of the night was long and lonely. Gone was the line I had refused to cross up to that point. And I could not leave as my vehicle was an hour away, so I lay in agony and disgrace in the bed of a thief.

Shattered Faith

As the sun rose, light peaked through the trees and into the window of the room. I got up and made my way to the bathroom. I felt broken, dirty, and ashamed. There was nothing I could do to change what had happened. I got ready so he could take me back to my pickup, but when I opened the door of that bathroom, nothing could have prepared me for the person he had become.

The kind flatterer was gone, replaced by a person who looked at me with disdain and contempt. I was a piece of trash in his eyes now, the snake in him revealed, and in his mind, it was time to throw me out. I had placed my trust in him, and he crushed my spirit. I felt rejected and alone, my faith shattered.

There was no love, kindness, or compassion there. He just wanted me gone. He was nothing like the funny, charming person who had enchanted me in class, and any hope I had of getting through this with a shred of dignity vanished. He had what he wanted, and he had taken something from me I could never recover. Like Eve in the garden of Eden, I had let down my guard, and a snake deceived me.

The snake's friend went along for the ride back to my pickup, knowing full well what had transpired. In the single cab pickup, I had no option but to sit between them. They joked with each other, and the snake's jokes were cruel and aimed at me. If he could have kicked me out without stopping, he would have. As it was, he threw my things to the pavement as I got out and then drove off. I never heard from or spoke to him again.

I drove home knowing I would never be the same. I had just become what people thought I was. The Enemy was quick to tell me that what had happened was all my fault. I was the one who put myself in that position. The burden of guilt was on me—I didn't speak up loud enough, and I deserved what I got.

In those hours of darkness, I fell further from grace than I ever thought possible. I kept it to myself, determined not to let anyone know what happened that night, not even my best friend. I couldn't bear the judgment. I was sure no one would find out, but when one of his friends asked me about it, I knew he was not only unashamed but proud of what he had done. I was a conquest, and he boasted about it.

I buried my shame and went forward as if nothing had happened. However, Satan reminded me often—the words *worthless, unclean,* and *unworthy* tormented me. I had to remember to breathe. Cast in a pit, I wallowed in self-pity. Indignity engulfed me as I continued down a road of self-loathing. I could not forgive myself, and Satan was not about to let me forget, so I perpetuated the cycle of more poor choices. The next one I found was an abuser and a user.

The abuser was neither charming nor funny. He tried to pretend he was an upstanding guy, though. Like a typical abuser, he would say or do horrible things and then try to redeem himself with a half-hearted gesture. I started dating him at the beginning of the fall semester of my second year at college. He expected me to drop everything for him and gave nothing but insults and criticism in return. He usually caught me when I was walking to math class, so I rarely went to class and eventually dropped it.

His idea of a date was going to the convenience store. I stayed in the pickup and found out later he had stolen something, usually alcohol. Since I drove him everywhere, I wonder who would have been in trouble for that crime? As I drove, he thought it funny to put his foot on top of mine and slam the gas pedal. We barreled down the road as I clung to the wheel, desperately trying to maintain control, a perfect mirror of my out-of-control life. He did drugs, drank, and yanked me around by my hair, but for some stupid reason, I was infatuated with him. He would do something charming or make me think he actually cared, and I was back under his control.

My self-esteem had fallen to an all-time low, and I was not eating much. During the week, I lived on two pieces of toast for breakfast and a candy bar and soda for lunch. My dinner was occasionally alcohol, but usually I just did not eat. When the weekend came, I binged and ate everything I could. One day my mom asked me if I was anorexic, and I stupidly took that as a compliment. I had a job in town soldering circuit boards, so I would work all day and then go to the college for my night classes; when I went to class, that is. My attendance in all my classes was lacking.

I was in my boyfriend's dorm room one night, and he was playing video games and completely ignoring me. There were several other boys in the room, and I was talking with them. For some reason, they decided they wanted to see me with my hair down. I had a bad perm and kept it pulled back until it grew out. Three of them tried to hold me down and remove my hair tie, but quickly their intentions changed. Panic gripped me and fight kicked in. I was not going to fall victim again. I resisted with everything I had in me, and when I was free, I saw my "boyfriend" still playing. The guys apologized to me, realizing they had gone too far, and he had not even bothered to look away from his game.

"Thanks for the help," I said, making sure he knew I was annoyed.

He returned my comment with, "You're not worth helping."

I stood there looking at him, processing what he had just said to me. I wasn't worth helping? It wasn't worth putting down a game controller to help me out of a bad situation? They were trying to disrobe me, and I wasn't worth saving from being gang raped?

I gathered my things and left, and he never even looked away from that stupid game. I walked to my pickup alone, and I felt completely unloved. I did not realize it at the time, but my attitude about life was beginning to change. The gouges in the lenses of my glasses were distorting my view on life. There was a stain placed on my soul that changed my perspective on the character of others.

Now you would think that an incident like that would be a turning point in any relationship, and a person with a thimble full of self-respect would have known better, but the next guy was just as bad. This one did not yank me around by my hair, but he was just as worthless and cruel. I let him monopolize my time as well, again placing my education second to him. After we had dated awhile, I knew he was cheating on me, but I let it slide. I put a smile on my face and feigned happiness.

Some of the other boys thought his deceit was funny, and they talked me into driving to town with them and going to the restaurant to confront him. Again, I was at a point at which I no longer cared, so I went along with the joke. When we were driving back, they decided to go out to the arena about a mile from the college. It was late, no one was around, and with no lights on, it was dark. I had yet again put myself in another risky situation. "Take me back," I said, "it's late, and I have to drive home." I was not playing around, and thankfully, they took me to my pickup. They were not pleased at all, and they treated me like the snake had treated me when he kicked me out of his truck. I didn't care if they were mad. I had grown weary of the games, gossip, and false accusations.

Unsaved boys can be ruthless. They will spin the truth to build themselves up. If they told the others what had actually happened, that they had been rejected, how would that have boosted their egos?

But I did have one ace up my sleeve with these boys, which was why nothing happened those nights in the dorm or at the arena. I had a friend who I dearly loved, and all these young men knew him and were afraid of him. I did not tell my friend what the snake had done because I feared what he might do to him. I would not have wanted my friend to get in trouble for one of my stupid mistakes.

The last dance I went to was with one of the best-looking guys from the college, and I had liked him the whole year. As usual, I drank too much, which led me to act stupid. I'm sure everyone thought the worst, but unfortunately, I did not care when I was in that state. When the dance was ending, we walked to the bar, and my friend walked over and put his arm across my date's shoulders. My friend leaned in, and I heard him say, "If she doesn't get home safe tonight, tomorrow I will hunt you down." He looked him in the eye and continued, "You don't want me to hunt you down."

There are so many ways that the Lord reaches down and helps us. He can use anyone or anything to intervene on our behalf. That doesn't mean we will not be wounded, but we have healing in the Savior. God is so patient and kind as He waits for us to turn to Him. It was my friend's words I heard, but it was the Lord's action. I definitely needed protection, not necessarily from this boy but from myself.

When we walked out to the parking lot, and I went to get in my pickup to drive home, my date was extremely nervous. I knew he was worried I would not get home safely, not because he cared about me, but because he was afraid of my friend. He tried to convince me to stay in town, and I could tell he wasn't happy when I got in my pickup and drove home. I didn't need him or his help because God was watching over me.

Like the sheep that wanders from the herd, I belonged to the Lord but did not fully understand His care over me. As I had done many times before, I drove home after drinking, and like the good Shepherd that He is, God watched over me. I had spent two years in college wandering away from the herd, but the Shepherd was gathering me back.

Psalm 121 says that we look to the mountains, wondering where our help comes from. It comes from the Lord. When I shut the door of my pickup that night, God shut the door of the toxic life I was living. He changed my course and set me on a different path, and for that I'm forever grateful.

Afterthought

I must admit, this was hard to write. The story is hard to tell, and I am not proud of it. As someone who sought affirmation, being treated like trash was the ultimate blow. While writing this out, I realized I had unhealed wounds. I had heaped condemnation upon myself for the scars of my past. I have fought the devil through this process, and I have had to face many fears. I faced the fear of judgment or pity, that people would shun me or worse. What if people do not believe me once they read this? However, those are lies from the Enemy. I wish I could say I was someone who never compromised my morals, and while the rumors were worse than the actuality, I still fell short. However, I cannot live in the shadow of others' opinions but only the redeeming grace of God.

Writing this has made me reflect on the people God placed in my life to protect me. There were so many things that could have happened because of my poor choices. My best girlfriend was someone who kept me out of trouble when I drank on more than one occasion. I am sorry that I made her think the worst of me, especially when she had every right to believe I was doing things I was not. Also, my best guy friend saved me by intimidation, and I am not sure he knows he did that.

Before I was led to tell my story, only two people knew what had happened to me that night, my husband and my oldest daughter. I told my husband because we tell each other those things, and I told my oldest daughter because I did not want her to make the same mistakes I had made. I found myself wondering why I kept this a secret from my family and friends. My conclusion is simply the fact that I was raised to "suck it up," and I am not a good victim. I am the girl who jumped up after my horse fell on me and got back on, hoping no one saw what happened. When we got to the branding pen, my ankle was so swollen I was unable to walk, but I still attempted to hide my injury. I am the pregnant woman who slipped on unmarked wet paint at the store, wrenched my back, and drove off without a complaint. Country kids are raised to be tough; that's just the way it is. And I have no issue with how I was raised, but I was also humiliated by what that boy did and how he had treated me, and I couldn't bear further degradation.

Stupid decisions like mine can linger indefinitely. Almost thirty years after this period in my life, I had one of these guys malign my character when he found out he was talking to a relative of mine. This was someone who had pursued a relationship with me, but I had no interest in dating him. I was floored that he was still bitter after almost three decades. This, however, is characteristic of the unsaved. How can someone forgive if they themselves have not been forgiven? Bitterness drove him to repeat gossip in his quest to hurt me. This made me even more thankful that my daughter had never opened herself up to such hateful slander. It also showed me how poor decisions can haunt you for a lifetime because there will always be people who want to stick a label on you and shame you. Typically, they are those who do not know God's redeeming grace and that Jesus washes us clean because He paid it all.

Recalling the details of that night, I found myself dealing with renewed hurt and shame, but God revealed something significant to me. It was something I had read before, but the Lord placed it on my heart as a new revelation and opened my eyes. An online article I found on erlc.com by Katie McCoy revealed that God does address sexual assault in the Bible. Deuteronomy 22:28–29 gives God's law concerning "date rape" because it talks about the virgin seized by a man and says, "then they are discovered." McCoy explains that the verse indicates the girl made the decision to be there; however, it was the man who chose to overwhelm her and violate her. God places the guilt on the man, the rapist; God does not want women exploited then thrown away. I encourage anyone suffering from the aftermath of rape, regardless of the circumstances, to read this article. The title is, "What does the Bible say about sexual assault?" by Katie McCoy. It helps to know how God views rape and how He regards the perpetrator of such an act.[3]

If you are a young woman in a destructive relationship, I encourage you to seek help. If you are a young woman facing pressure to have sex out of wedlock, I pray that you will refrain from caving to the demand. Someone who genuinely loves you will be willing to wait for you; they need to cherish you as God does. There is a reason why God calls us to purity and to abstain from sexual immorality, and it is because it hurts us at the core of our being—it hurts our soul. Therefore, when something so irreplaceable and precious is either given or taken by force, it scars us internally, and we have pain that God never intended for us. These are wounds that only God can heal. It is a testament to how vital our identity is in Christ because when we do not understand how precious we are to Him, we do not place the appropriate value on ourselves. God's love is like no other.

As I was writing this, Satan tried to convince me I was still unworthy and guilty. I had to remind myself of one of God's promises, which is, "Submit yourselves therefore to God. Resist the devil, and he will flee from you," James 4:7 (KJV). As I submitted myself to God by doing what He called me to do, the Enemy tried to keep me from His will. Satan will do everything he can to try and convince believers that he has power over us, but the real power is inside us, because when we are saved, God is in us.

The hardest thing I had to do in this process of writing my story was to forgive. Forgiveness is hard! I had to not only forgive the young men in my past, but I needed to also forgive myself, because these were unhealed wounds I rediscovered. Without forgiveness for all of us, there can be no healing. It does not change what happened, but with true forgiveness comes freedom. Chances are the person who raped me does not even remember what he did because it meant nothing to him. The others treated me the way I allowed them to because I didn't stand up for myself when I should have. If I hold on to hate, I am not hurting them—I am hurting myself. God will deal with them when the time comes, and the only power I have is to move forward in faith and forgiveness. I also have a responsibility to pray for these boys who are now men. "But I say, love your enemies! Pray for those who persecute you!" (Matthew 5:44 NLT)

If you see yourself in my story in any way and are struggling with your identity, I want to encourage you to see yourself the way God sees you. If you need help, please seek counseling. If you are reading this and have not asked Jesus Christ to be your Savior, my prayer is that you will make that choice. The Lord is the only One worthy of your faith. "It is the Lord who goes before you. He will be with you; he will not leave you or forsake you. Do not fear or be dismayed" (Deuteronomy 31:8 ESV).

Faith Lesson: When we place our faith in the people and things of this earth, we will be let down. Only God can save and redeem. We are made whole through Christ alone.

Ranch Talk

I grew up on a working cattle ranch. We ran about 350 head of mother cows on almost 30,000 acres. In late spring, we would gather the cattle and brand the new calves. The purpose is to mark the calves so that it is clear what ranch they belong to, who owns them, protects them, and cares for them. When we accept Jesus as our Savior, it is like being branded for the Lord. We do not receive a physical mark, but we are marked. We are under the protection of the One True King, and He cares for us. "The Lord knows those who are his," 2 Timothy 2:19 (ESV) tells us. He knows we are His because we have His seal or brand (2 Corinthians 1:21–22).

If you have not asked Jesus to be your Savior, then you are not His, and you are not under the Lord's protection. When you are ready, I encourage you to ask the Lord into your life. However, you need to acknowledge you have sinned and turn from that sin. You can do this by praying the following prayer of salvation.

Prayer

Heavenly Father, I come before You broken and in need of redemption. I acknowledge that I have sinned against You, Lord, and I ask for Your forgiveness. I know that You are the Savior and that You died on the cross for me, and I believe this in my heart. I call on Your name, Jesus, please help me live a new life in You, and be my Lord and Savior, amen.

Study

1. Who is Jesus? Jesus tells us in the book of John. Look up His seven "I am" statements in the Bible version of your choice, and write out what it says about who Jesus is. (An easy way to do this is through a Bible app, such as Bible Hub, Blue Letter Bible, or BibleGateway. You can access many versions and even compare them next to each other. Try it!)

    John 6:35, 41, 48, 51   I am _____

    John 8:12   I am _____

    John 10:7, 9   I am _____

    John 11:25   I am _____

    John 10:11, 14   I am _____

    John 14:6   I am _____

    John 15:1, 5   I am _____

2. Now write seven "I am" statements of your own. I will help you with the first one:

    I am **forgiven** _____

    I am _____

    I am _____

    I am _____

    I am _____

    I am _____

    I am _____

3. Read your "I am" statements every day to remember who you are in Christ, perhaps writing them on a notecard to keep them close to you.

Moving Forward in Faith

The angel of the Lord encamps all around
those who fear Him,
And delivers them.
Psalm 34:7 NKJV

"I sat on the side of the road in the cab of the semi, alone, in the dark. *I have to drive this thing*, I thought, *I have no other choice.* I fought back panic as I assessed my situation. I had two choices—sit on the side of the road, or take control of my fear and drive this truck."

Long, Lonely Night

I met my husband Link right after my twentieth birthday. He was back on his family's ranch because his grandfather had passed away. Our introduction took place by way of a blind date. I remember I was in the backyard when he arrived. I peeked around the corner, not believing another girl was dropping him off, but I found out later it was his sister. By the end of that hot August night in 1989, we had made a connection, and three months later we were married. He worked on his family ranch when we first were married, but it quickly became apparent that we were not going to survive on that wage. He went searching for a job, and by the beginning of December of that year, we were in a semitruck hauling produce from Nogales, Arizona, to downtown Los Angeles. Any couple who can survive the honeymoon period of their marriage in the cab of a semi should be able to handle anything, right? My slamming door was the zipper on the sleeper curtain. Zip, zip, zip!

Most people have a plan for their lives, but we had no thoughts about our future. We ignorantly opted to live day by day, which happened to be in the cab of the semi driving endlessly down the road. Truck drivers do not have a great reputation, and it has gotten worse over the years.

There was a time in American history when truck drivers and the trucking culture had some popularity, and the general public looked at this industry in a positive light. Kids idolized truckers, and the portrayal of truck drivers in songs romanticized the lifestyle. Many considered them to be "good Samaritans" of the road because they were willing to stop for people in need of help. The reputation of truckers declined when movies started portraying them as antagonists and serial killers.[4] In 2009, the FBI released a study which speculated that many cold case murders were likely the work of long-haul truck drivers.[5]

However, there are still upstanding drivers on the road today, and we are still friends with some of them. Let's just say that in general, the industry does not uphold standards in which a Christian couple should immerse themselves. Link was one of those kids from the 70s who idolized the profession, and he started driving a truck right out of high school. It was something he loved doing.

I have no statistics on the number of truck drivers who are serial killers, but it is an industry that involves a lot of drug use and human trafficking. So for a girl who grew up on a ranch, this realization was a big culture shock. Life in big cities was also shocking with the congestion and noise, but adding in the sin that runs rampant in those areas and that industry, I must say, I was out of my element. Those boys in college had nothing on this life.

We typically hauled three loads a week, which meant we were nonstop driving back and forth. We drove what they call a cabover; those are the trucks that have no hood, so the front of the semi is flat. Since the cab sits over the engine, you must climb up into them, and when you open the door, you are looking at the floorboard area. We pulled a reefer trailer, which is just a trailer with a refrigerated unit on the front, and we could haul up to 60,000 pounds of cargo.

There was one trip that will be etched in my memory forever. We loaded in Nogales as usual, 60,000 pounds of cucumbers; we could not legally carry any more weight. It is typical to get finished loading in the late afternoon, which always meant you would be driving most of the night. It was imperative to be at the market when they opened to off-load, or you ran the risk of the load not getting accepted, which was not good. If we were late and the load was refused, we had to find other buyers before we could head back to Nogales.

On this day, the sun had gone down, and we were about seventy miles past Phoenix on I-10 headed to California when Link needed sleep. The trailer we were pulling had an issue with its marker lights, which are the lights that go around the top. There was a short in the wiring, and they would go out with no warning. The only way to know if they had gone out was noticing it in the mirror. We would always swap drivers going down the road. I would take the wheel, and Link would climb out of the seat, and I would slip in. It was seamless, and no one knew we were swapping.

I settled in to drive, and Link took his shoes off and climbed into the sleeper for rest. I would typically drive until we started getting into heavy traffic, and then he would take over again. The truth was,

I had a license to drive but did not run a logbook and was not on the insurance; technically, the owner of the company did not know about this, so I should not have been in the driver's seat. However, there I was.

Unbeknownst to me, the marker lights on the trailer went out. I saw the Highway Patrol in the median when the semi lights illuminated off the vehicle but was not speeding and continued undaunted. It surprised me when the red and blue lights flashed in the side mirror. Struck with fear, I started yelling for Link to wake up as I slowed to pull off the road. Panic increased, and my voice elevated. Link needed to get out of the sleeper and into the driver's seat before the officer reached the door. We switched places at the very last second, but Link did not get his shoes back on. Well, the officer took it upon himself to open the door, and the first thing he saw was Link's socks. Having no shoes on, along with the fact that we were "truck drivers," made him a bit uncertain of the situation.

He took Link's license and walked back to his car. Link put his shoes on and followed him, and I waited patiently in the sleeper of the truck. It seemed like an eternity as I sat and waited, and I was surprised when the passenger door abruptly opened, and the officer climbed into the cab.

"I am arresting your husband," he said, "so I need to see your driver's license." He was sharp, curt, and matter of fact.

I was stunned by what he just said, and I searched for my purse, my mind racing. I was not sure what to do. Fumbling through my wallet, I pulled out my license and handed it to the officer. He looked it over and gave it back.

"You can come back and talk to him if you want," he said, as he climbed out of the cab.

I gathered myself, and sliding from the bed to the passenger seat, I clutched the handle and climbed down the steps on the side of the cab. I walked behind him, and when we reached the patrol car, I could not believe what I saw. There was Link, his arms behind him, handcuffs on his wrists. For the first time in my life, I saw someone I loved in handcuffs, and reality set in.

"Just get in the truck," he said, "and drive it back to the truck stop in Phoenix." I heard his words, but I was in shock.

"Wait. . . what?" That is what I *wanted* to say, but instead, I began to cry. Sob is a better word, one of those ugly cries. I could not help it. Here I was, a twenty-year-old ranch girl on the side of the road, seventy miles outside of Phoenix, in a semi, as an officer was about to drive off with my arrested husband handcuffed in the back seat. Who had I married?

I knew Link had prayed for salvation with the pastor of my oldest sister's church before our wedding day, but of course, he had a life before he met me. Just like myself, his previous life was not the most moral and upstanding existence. He had lived with a woman for several years, and since he drove a truck, he was away from home most of the time. That meant if he got a ticket, he sent it to her, expecting she would pay it when they had money, only this time she didn't. He knew he had an outstanding brake citation in California, but he believed that was the only one. Being young and dumb, he ignored the notices because he did not feel it was his responsibility.

I could not stop crying, but when I watched the lights of the patrol car disappear, I came to my senses, ran back to the open door of the truck, and climbed into the cab. Locking the doors, I remember sitting there for a minute. Now I have never liked scary movies, but if ever there was an excellent plot for a scary movie, I think I was in it. It was quiet, except for the occasional car driving past at high speed. Since I typically just took over for Link while driving down the highway, I had only gone through all the gears once or twice. I looked up and saw the CB radio. Grabbing it, I clicked the mic and called out the name of our trucking company. I was hoping that someone who drove for the same company would be in range and would help me. There was no response, and I was unable to hide the panic in my voice when I tried again. Nothing, no one responded.

I sat on the side of the road in the cab of the semi, alone, in the dark. *I have to drive this thing,* I thought, *I have no other choice.* I fought back panic as I assessed my situation. I had two choices—sit on the side of the road, or take control of my fear and drive this truck.

As someone who now panics when I forget my phone, I am not sure how I survived those days before cell phones.

I took a breath and made myself stop crying. *I can do this,* I thought. *I have to do this.* I had no other choice unless I just sat on the side of the road. I looked down at the gearshift. I had to go through thirteen gears with a splitter in the middle. Another deep breath, and I pushed the clutch to the floor; placing my hand on the stick, I put the truck in gear. It was about 10:00 p.m., and traffic was minimal at this hour, especially so far outside the city. I slowly eased back onto the highway, revving the engine and shifting to my next gear as the semi crawled forward. I repeated the process, and as I gained speed, I started to relax some, and my confidence increased.

I moved forward in faith, thinking only of the next step, the next task. I refrained from dwelling on the "what ifs" of my predicament. I had to drive about a mile up the road to find an overpass to go back to Phoenix. I tried calling on the CB a few more times, but I gave up hope when there was no response.

I got turned around and headed back to Phoenix. I made it through all the gears again, but knew my biggest challenge was still ahead of me. The truck stop that I headed to was small, and at night it would be impossible to find a parking spot. I knew I would have to park on the street, and I wasn't sure how far I would have to walk. I pushed the thought away. I had to take this one step at a time.

Finally, I exited the interstate and could see the truck stop. The lights illuminated the parking area, and I could tell it was full. Just past the last entrance was a narrow road, so I turned down it, hoping to find a place to park that was not too far from the store and trucker's lounge. The street was poorly lit and engulfed in shadows of darkness. The only light came from the truck stop, and it cast dim, patchy light onto the street. Several other trucks lined the curb. I drove past them until I finally came to an end and was able to park. I turned the engine off and sat in the quiet darkness. I could see my destination in the side mirror, but I had a long walk. This area was not a good one. People hang out around truck stops for drugs and other unsavory things. Now I was going to have to gather my courage and walk the gauntlet.

I had $250 in cash and a $250 Comchek to cover expenses. I pulled the keys from the ignition and placed them in my pocket in case someone grabbed my purse. I did not want to be stranded. I opened the door and dropped down to the asphalt below. I shut the door, and the loud noise echoed down the street. Having left the safety of the cab, I looked at my destination and the walk I had ahead of me. The dimly lit street was daunting with its dark, dangerous shadows. I bowed my head, knowing I needed courage, and with fear increasing inside me, I knew I had to move. So with a silent prayer, I stepped forward in faith that God would protect me.

Pastor Greg Laurie is the pastor for Harvest Christian Fellowship. I watch him on YouTube all the time. He has a two-part series entitled "Angels and Demons." The sermon's message is the biblical accounts of instances in which angels come to protect humans or communicate a message from God. Laurie references the story of Elisha and his servant Gehazi when in 2 Kings 6:17, Elisha prayed that God would open the servant's eyes so he could see the army of the Lord. When God opened Gehazi's eyes, he saw the horses and chariots of fire, and they were surrounding Elisha.[6] There are numerous verses in the Bible that reference angels safeguarding and assisting humans on earth. I firmly believe there were angels with me on that night.

Here I was, a prime target. A young woman, alone on a dim side street in the middle of the night. Add the sketchy area, and you have the making of a plot for a CSI episode. I am a relatively fast-paced walker, so at an unrelenting pace, I started toward the truck stop. I could hear a group of men talking, and I knew I would be walking right in front of them. Undaunted, I put my head down and continued my mission. I crossed the street, unsure of what was about to happen. I expected something to happen, but as I glanced at them out of the corner of my eye, they didn't seem to notice me. I did not slow down, my thoughts fixed on my destination. It was surreal. I was sure they could see me because I could see them, but they never looked at me or said a word.

I reached the store, breathing a sigh of relief as I stepped into safety. *Thank You, Lord*, was my thought, as I headed to the counter for help. On the verge of tears, I walked up, expecting a sympathetic ear. My hopeful expectation dissipated when the cashier looked at me with disdain. I explained the entire situation, expressing my need to cash the Comchek I had in my possession. She was rude and unpleasant, refusing to help, and she dismissed me and called for the next person in line.

I started to cry again and slipped into the bathroom to hide my distress. At this point, it was about midnight, and I was running on adrenaline. I knew if I slowed down, I would quit. Determined, I left the bathroom and walked to the payphones to look up a number for a taxi. I stood outside and waited for the cab to arrive, and when it pulled up, I slipped into the back seat. It was my first experience in a taxi. I didn't know what to expect but hoped to find someone sympathetic to my plight. The driver was friendly, and I explained my predicament to him. He was rather compassionate; we talked the entire drive, and when we pulled into the Sheriff's station, I felt better. I paid him, stepped out of the cab, and watched him drive off.

The poorly lit parking lot was empty, and it was around one in the morning, so no one was around the station. I had to explain over an intercom the purpose of the visit. I was startled by the loud buzz at the door, which made me jump. I grabbed the handle, opened the door, and stepped into a small room. The clerk sat behind bulletproof glass, and it was difficult to know if she could hear what I was asking her. I explained my circumstance and why I was standing in front of her at one in the morning. When she looked Link up in her system, I was able to get a clear picture of the situation. A logbook violation that initially was a $25 fine was now, with penalties and interest, $500. She would not take the Comchek and offered no advice or assistance.

Discouraged, I walked outside to find a payphone and call the taxi company again so I could get back to the truck stop. To my dismay, there were no payphones at the Sheriff's station. The area I was in was rural, the road that went past the station was dark, and there were few streetlights. I stepped onto the street and looked in both directions but saw nothing that promised a payphone. I opted to head west since that was the way I came when I was in the cab. It was the first time I was able to put some thought toward my circumstance, and fear began to well up inside me. I found myself thinking of all the evil I might encounter, and the Enemy took the opportunity I offered him. Fear took hold, my heart beating rapidly and adrenaline pumping through my body, which made me jump at every noise. I could see a grocery store in front of me. It looked abandoned, but I still ran toward it.

At the front of the building was a row of payphones, and I looked around nervously as I walked toward them. I kept thinking, *If the wrong car full of the wrong people came along, it could be horrible.* Picking up the phone, I decided to call my mom. I let her know about my situation just in case I disappeared. The second call I made was to the cab company.

It was the same taxi, and I was relieved to see the same driver. He dropped me off at the truck stop, and at this moment, I knew what

I would have to do next. I needed to call the owner of the company, Link's boss.

It was after 2:00 a.m. now, and when I picked the phone up, there was a knot in my stomach; I did not want to do this. When Gary answered the phone, I sheepishly explained the situation.

He was gracious and somewhat surprised that I could drive the truck. We forged a plan. However, the only option we had involved driving the semi, which I assured him I could do. I hung up the phone and realized what came next. I would have to walk back to the truck in the dark. I recalled my fear. Walking back to the semi would be more dreadful because I would have to fumble with the key when I reached the truck. I would have no light, so I would have to feel around to get the key in the lock and open the door. That would leave me vulnerable to anyone coming up behind me. My inner chicken reminded me of the danger.

But I reminded myself of how faithful God had been through this whole ordeal, so I pulled the key out of my pocket, clutched it in my hand, and started the walk back to the semi. I did not want to have to find the key when I got there. I saw no one on the trip back, and when I reached the door, I opened it as quickly as I could and climbed up to safety. I sat in silence and assessed my situation. I had to drive this semi again.

I drove around the block and got back on the freeway heading west. I had to drive twenty-six miles to another truck stop to get a Comchek from Gary, in my name this time, and then go and get Link sprung from jail.

After nine hours of constant stress, I was grateful when it finally ended; however, we still had 60,000 pounds of cucumbers that needed a new buyer, and that fell to us. I was thankful that God brought me through that night. There were so many things that could have gone wrong, so many unspeakable things that could have happened, but He protected me and kept me safe.

A few weeks after the Phoenix incident, when we were driving from Los Angeles heading north. We had to cross Tejon Pass on I-5, which is affectionately called "The Grapevine." It drops 2,613 feet in 11.6 miles in descent toward the San Joaquin Valley. To be accurate, the Grapevine portion of the pass is the northern end, which is five-and-a-half miles of steep grade; it has two runaway ramps that get put to use often.[7]

That day, the trailer was empty, and Link was driving relatively fast. I pointed out the speed limit sign to him, which was on a gantry stretched over the road. It was large and prominent. With the Phoenix incident fresh in my mind, and the fact that we knew he had an outstanding violation in California, I was a bit aggravated when he told me it was an "advisory" speed. The sign showed 35 mph; however, it was yellow, so I gave him the benefit of the doubt, because it seemed ridiculous. It was mere minutes after I pointed that out when we saw red and blue lights in the mirror.

Another truck driver was following Link, and the CHP (California Highway Patrol) car was pulling both semis over. The officer that got out looked like Johnny Law, by the book, and he jumped onto the step of our truck and said, "I'll start with your logbook, boy." Then he jumped down and walked to the truck behind us. When Link looked at me, I was sobbing uncontrollably, terrified I was going to have to drive the semi off the mountain. I remember him saying, "Oh, like that doesn't make us look guilty of something." I was unable to stop crying, trying to catch my breath, and my body was shaking.

"I don't want to drive this truck off this mountain!" I said, a bit elevated at this point. That endless night was playing in my head, and I had no desire to go through that again. Thankfully Johnny Law was with the other driver, and we had his rookie. The young officer just looked at Link's license and logbook and wrote out a ticket.

Afterthought

Several thoughts were going through my head as I wrote this, and the first and most important was, "Do not call your mom at 2:00 a.m. and scare her half to death." I think about it, and I cannot believe I was the cause of Mom's sleepless night of worry. Worse yet, I do not think I called her to let her know I was safe. It was difficult to make calls back then, but that is no excuse. I found out later my mom had called the Sheriff's station and chewed them out for leaving me stranded on the side of the road. I cannot imagine she went back to bed, and I should have called her when things were under control. What was I thinking?

I was also realizing we looked like real losers. Well, all I can say is we were incredibly young and dumb. The citation Link had in California was for brakes, which he had to get fixed before he could leave the inspection station. The citation was the company's responsibility because it was an issue with the truck.

However, it is incredible to look back and see how faithful God was and the protection He provided. I honestly believe His angels protected me that night as I walked to the truck stop. There is no other explanation for why the men on that street did not even seem to see me, because if they had, they would have at least said something to me. I was a young girl walking with a purse with cash in it, on a dark side street, in a sketchy area, and I know God was guarding me. He had to be. I did not feel afraid until I let fear take control, when I chose to doubt.

Faith is a conscious choice. You need to profess your trust in God. The Bible tells us that God protects His children; however, that does not mean His children can act in ways or participate in actions outside of His will and still expect protection. The Lord may indeed protect us through unconscionable choices, but I do not recommend testing Him. The Bible warns about trying God in Matthew 4:7 (ESV), when Jesus replied, "Again it is written, 'You shall not put the Lord your God to the test.'"

Faith Lesson: The things that God allows us to endure may be difficult, but He teaches us how to persevere through trials and grow spiritually as we learn to put our faith in Him.

Ranch Talk

Growing up on a ranch, we had a lot of things to do to keep us busy. In Arizona, we have hot summer days, and my sister and I did not have a traditional swimming pool. Therefore, the only option we had was a cement tank on the hill above our house. The tank was an open cement structure that was about four feet deep, six feet wide, and ten feet long.

Ranch kids are reasonably tough and tend to do things city kids would not do. This tank had thick algae that covered the walls, so the water was always green. We would fish the dead birds off the top before we climbed in, and we just had to deal with the slime and bugs. When swimming, there is no way to avoid swallowing some of the water, so this was a test of our immune systems. Thankfully, it never made us sick. The worst was when we swam in the tank at Mud Springs, and Dad knew we had swum there because a dead deer popped up from the bottom. In my mind, this measure of my immune system would be similar to testing God; however, testing God is far worse, so I wouldn't recommend doing that.

If there are areas in your life where you feel you may be testing God, you can pray for the Lord to remove that from you. Pray not only for forgiveness, but if it is a sin that is holding you captive, pray for deliverance from it.

Prayer

Heavenly Father, I come before You to ask for forgiveness for anything I have been doing outside Your will. I ask, Father, that You would reveal sins that have been controlling me and that You would remove any bonds the Enemy has placed on me. I pray this in Jesus' name, amen.

Study

Satan looks to entice us with sin, just as he tried to tempt Jesus in the wilderness (Matthew 4:1–10). The Enemy is a master at temptation, but he cannot stand against God.

I had a flatterer pursuing me at one point; Satan knows our weaknesses. However, when I prayed that God would take that from me, the Lord revealed something in him that instantly doused any attraction I had toward him. God is faithful, and He hears our prayers.

As Christians, we have the Holy Spirit who indwells us and is our internal compass. We each have specific morals that are core values, and as followers of Christ, these standards often go against worldly core values.

1. Look up Galatians 5:22–23 and write down the fruit of the Spirit. _____

_____

_____

_____

_____

2. Now, write down your core values in the table below. Examples of this are honesty, loyalty, wisdom, knowledge, peace, and so on. If you need more examples, you can search "core values list" on the internet.

3. Sin compromises our values and places us outside the will of God. After you write down your core values, write down any sins or desires that compromise those values. Be honest with God and yourself. In the prayer above, you asked God to reveal those sins to you, so now is the time to really listen and reflect, to soul search.

Core Value	Sin or Design Outside of God's Will
Example: Generosity	Greed/making money an idol

4. Pray the above prayer again, and this time name each sin as you ask the Lord to remove those bonds.

Faith through Fire

For it is written,
"He will command his angels
concerning you, to guard you."
Luke 4:10 ESV

"It took me a moment to realize where I was, and I tapped Link on the shoulder. 'Link, someone is banging on the door,' I said, not awake enough to understand. Then I heard his words, 'Your truck is on fire!'"

Moving On

It is impossible as mere humans to have complete control over anything in life. Just as I could not control what happened the night I sat on the side of the road in the semi, I have no control of the future. We will face trials in our lives intended to make us stronger in our faith in the Lord. Some testing is of our integrity and can seem minor, but other trials show us that God controls everything, even fire.

In the late spring of 1990, we changed trucking companies. We met our best friends when we started driving a truck, and when they moved to another company, we followed them. With summer approaching, we hauled seafood from the California coast up to Washington. The change in scenery was terrific, but the company's owner tended to cut corners when it came to repairs on the trucks. We had issues with brakes, tires, and our air conditioner, to name a few.

When hauling from San Francisco we had some time before loading, so Link and I had an opportunity to be tourists for a few hours. We dropped our trailer at a truck stop and went to see the Golden Gate Bridge. Our brakes were so bad at this point that when we parked, Link had to put rocks around the tires so the truck would not roll away. The brakes were terrible, and the tires were bald; we were a real class act.

We drove without air conditioning in the semi, which is not a huge deal up north, but it is miserable when driving across the Arizona desert in summer. With temperatures averaging 107° with a record high in 1990 of 122°, you could say we got hot.[8] Our only reprieve was stopping and getting in the refrigerated trailer, which made it worse when you had to get back on the road. Link never said anything harsh to the owner. He would mention it and ask to get it fixed, but nothing happened.

On one trip, we were in Kent, Washington, and had some extra time and decided to go to a movie, so we dropped the trailer and bobtailed to the theater. When we came out of the theater, it was late afternoon, and when Link turned the key, the truck would not start. A rock was keeping us from rolling off, the tires were bald, and now it would not start. At about this time, a Highway Patrol officer drove up, and she was willing to help us. I was embarrassed, and I remember trying to stand in front of the drive tires, thinking I could hide them. Then I looked down at the rock that served as our brake and hoped she would not notice it. She had to have seen all of those issues, but she was kind enough just to jumpstart the truck and leave without giving us a citation for the numerous safety violations. I am certain Link's boss would have expected us to pay those fines, and we did not have the money for something like that. In retrospect, the semi should not have been on the road, especially going over the mountains.

The mountain pass on I-5 between California and Oregon is called the Siskiyou Summit, and it drops 2,000 feet in six miles when headed north. The high elevation coupled with dangerous curves makes it extremely challenging, and in winter, the pass is often shut down entirely due to weather conditions.[9]

In the early nineties, anyway, truck drivers called the Siskiyou Summit "Ashland Pass" because the Port of Entry is on the north side in Ashland, Oregon. I came to dread going over this pass due to the brake issues on the semi.

At that time, semitrucks did not have self-adjusting brakes like they do today, so drivers needed to adjust the brakes about once a week. However, because our brake pads were so worn, Link had to do this more often. When it was time to drive down the north side of Ashland Pass, he would get out, and with a wrench, he would have to crank down the pads so they would make contact with the drum. There were ten hubs, and this truck only had four that had some pad left for contact—two on the front wheels of the semi, and two on the trailer. The last time we went down the north side of this pass with the brakes in this condition, they were smoking so bad Link had to pull into a rest area about halfway down so they could cool. That was a wakeup call, and Link finally demanded the brakes to be fixed before we drove it anywhere else. Our lives and the lives of others on the road with us were in danger. We were young and too afraid to stand up to the owner. My husband and our friends were not inclined to complain, and the owner took advantage of us.

The friends we followed to this company are brothers, and their dad and stepmom lived in Seattle, so we tried to lay over there whenever we could. If we all unloaded late Friday, it was typically too late to get loaded for our backhaul, and we would get to wait until Monday. This scenario was uncommon, but when everything worked, it was a blessing. These times are some of my fondest memories.

One of our loads was going to a warehouse in Kent, Washington, and we arrived there around midnight. It was late fall, and it was cold. To run the heater when parked, Link would use the throttle lock to rev the engine to around 1,100 RPMs; this is something drivers do because it is better for the motor. The warehouse would not open until morning. Exhausted, we squeezed into the twin bed and were out like lights.

Link is a very sound sleeper, and when he is in a deep sleep, the world could collapse around him and he wouldn't notice. I slept lighter, but it had to be something drastic to wake me.

It took a bit for my mind to register the noise. I heard it, and it slowly began to penetrate my state of unconsciousness. There was someone frantically knocking at the door of the truck. It took me a moment to realize where I was, and I tapped Link on the shoulder. "Link, someone is banging on the door," I said, not awake enough to understand. Then I heard the stranger's words, "Your truck is on fire!"

"Link, someone is yelling at the door," I repeated, my voice elevated.

Link sat up and when he heard fire, he jumped into action and got out of the semi in just his underwear, no other clothes, and no shoes. When they lifted the hood, flames shot in the air. I was trying to get dressed, still not completely aware of how dire our situation was. Link opened the door and climbed back in to get clothes on. I could tell he was rattled when he told me to get out of the truck.

I quickly finished dressing and stepped out onto the dark black asphalt. The cold air felt thick, and I noticed that the street had a blanket of heavy smoke. It was early in the morning, and there was no activity.

When the gravity of the situation hit us, we realized we had been minutes from death. We had recently heard of another driver whose truck had caught fire, and he died due to toxic smoke from the dashboard as it smoldered. When the emergency was under control, we stood talking with the man who had helped us. "Something woke me up," he said, "and I had an urgent feeling I needed to get to work." He had arrived at the warehouse an hour earlier than he needed to, and when turning down the street, he saw the smoke and knew our truck was on fire. What a sobering thought, knowing that God rescued us from burning up in the semi that morning. We had about five minutes before we would have died from smoke inhalation.

Pastor Greg Laurie's message on angels and demons says that we may talk to angels and never know it; they can appear to us as humans in everyday life.[10] I think in the wee hours of that morning, we may have met our angel. None of us remember seeing that man again when delivering to that warehouse. I believe it was a miracle that he was there to get us out of that truck, but ultimately, the glory goes to God.

All of us were laid over in Seattle that weekend. At the time, neither Link nor I grasped the magnitude of that blessing. We carried on as if nothing extraordinary had happened. We did not give God enough glory for what He had done for us that morning, for what He had saved us from.

As winter approached, we stopped driving from California to Washington and returned to the Nogales to Los Angeles route. I was growing weary of living in a semi, and in January of 1991, I decided I wanted to stay home. At this time, home was a fifth-wheel trailer parked in an RV lot next to the house our friends rented. I was happy to stay in one spot. I decided to go to a trade school, and Link continued driving.

Link drove for a few more months, then God changed our course again.

Afterthought

I look back at this time, and I cannot believe we had so much adventure. We put up with more than we should have and allowed others the ability to place our lives in danger. However, this just further highlights the protection that God put over us.

I wish I would have paid more attention to the man who got us up and out of the truck that morning, and if I had fully comprehended the danger we were in, I could have acknowledged his action better. Being young and thinking we are invincible means there is often a lack of appreciation for many circumstances we face. When God heaped blessings on us, I had such an immature spirit that I did not always discern it was God's grace. I knew enough to realize He had protected us, but I did not grasp the depth of His love—God saved us!

People who do not know God attribute moments of protection or good fortune to "luck" or "the universe," but the Bible clearly states that God is in control of everything. Therefore, to see any event in your life as happenstance is to deny God's sovereignty and His "omni" attributes—He is all-powerful, all-present, and all-knowing.[11]

In Psalm 139:2–12, David acknowledges that God knows what he is doing and thinking, the words he will speak, and the places he will go. God guides David and protects him. He cannot flee from the Lord, nor hide from Him. Like David, I know God saved us that night, and I know I am under His protection every day.

Faith Lesson: God sends angels to intervene for us just as God sent an angel to close the mouths of the lions for Daniel. I believe the Lord sent an angel to get us out of that fire—either the man knocking on our door or whoever he said woke him to go to work early.

Ranch Talk

Growing up, I did many things that compromised my well-being, but God was always there to protect me. I had a mean, flea-bitten gray horse I had named "Banjo." My Uncle Alvin called him "The

Banjo String" because he was very narrow chested. He always said it looked like both front legs came out of the same hole. I was leaving the house, and the horses were in the shipping corrals watering. I was in college at this time, and I was not riding much, so when I saw that the horses were in, I got nostalgic and walked out to see Banjo. There were about fifteen horses, and among them was a broodmare we called Maude. She was a nice mare, but other than the occasional pat when I walked by her, I had never paid her much attention.

I walked over to my old "friend" and went to touch him on the shoulder. With no warning, he lunged at me, teeth bared and aiming for my face. It was so unexpected; I did not react fast enough, and I felt his teeth touch my cheek. But thankfully, his plan was derailed. At the very second he was getting ready to bite down on my cheek, Maude pinned her ears and charged him. She bit him in the shoulder and knocked him off course. The bite would have been devastating for my face. I was left questioning what had propelled that mare into motion and sidetracked Banjo's strike. The only explanation is the grace of God. Nonbelievers will likely want to speculate about the herd mentality and drone on about the equine's nature. But to me, the answer is simple: God. He moved that mare at the precise second she needed to move to keep me from that, and to the Lord I give the glory.

God protects His children every day, and often we do not even realize how close we are to calamity. The Lord shielded me from something that would have affected me the rest of my life, just as He did that morning in the semi, and I am so thankful for that. God tells us it is acceptable to pray for His protection. Psalm 143:9 (CSB) says, "Rescue me from my enemies, Lord; I come to you for protection."

Prayer

Lord, I come before You aware there are many dangers in this world. I acknowledge that I have no power over the things that may attempt to overtake me. I pray, heavenly Father, that You would guide me and protect me as I seek Your will for my life, and as I seek shelter under Your wings. I pray You will keep evil from me, my faithful Protector. Because you are my Father, I will have no fear. In Jesus' name I pray, amen.

Study

God does not want us to worry, and we are told repeatedly in the Bible not to fear. I used to wake up in the middle of the night in a panic, and I would have to get up because I could not go back to sleep. I finally realized I needed to sincerely pray for God's will in my life because He promises to sustain us. I spent many years afraid to pray for His will because I mistakenly believed it would not be what I wanted, and I knew best. But God knows what is best for us, so why wouldn't we want His will? It is His will that blesses us beyond all measure.

Since God is sovereign, He knows what is best in every situation. I encourage you to work through the following exercise to help gain control of fear.

1. God is omnipresent (everywhere at all times), omniscient (knows everything), and omnipotent (has power over everything). Read Psalm 139:2–12 to get a better understanding of how God is always with us.

2. Look up Psalm 91:5–6 and write down what God tells us not to fear in this verse. _____
   _____
   _____

3. Now, write down things you are inclined to fear and worry about in the chart.

4. Write down the cause of this fear in the chart. Think about it and pray about it. Why are you afraid of this? What caused you to be afraid of this?

5. Now write down who has control over this. Is it you or God?

Read my story and example below for help in filling out the chart.

WORRY	CAUSE OF FEAR	WHO?

Look up and write down Joshua 1:9. _____

_____

_____

_____

Now, cover it in prayer!

A couple of years ago, my daughter and son-in-law took my grandkids to the lake. My grandson Kail was four, and my granddaughter Kadence was two years old. I had an ominous fear that I just could not shake. It was not about anything in particular; I just had an uneasy feeling. I did not say anything to my daughter because I did not want to make her worry.

I decided to confide in my husband, asking him to cover the weekend in prayer. The whole weekend I prayed every time it came to mind, which was often that weekend. The kids did not have cell service at the lake, so it was Monday when my daughter Taylor called.

"Everyone is safe, right? I have had a bad feeling and have been praying all weekend." This statement was the first thing out of my mouth, and it was met with silence.

"Well, that is interesting," Taylor said, "because Kadence had a near-drowning experience."

I was floored, and when I heard the story, I was so grateful to God.

My precious granddaughter was swimming with other kids in a shallow area close to their camp. Taylor was with her, and because Kadence could not move well in her life vest and she was sitting there, she let her take it off. She had only had it off a few minutes when a microburst came through the camp, and everyone started grabbing for flying items. Instinctively, my daughter tried to grab an object and was away from the pool of water when she heard one of the little girls saying, "Kadence is drowning."

When Taylor looked, she saw that Kadence had floated out to deeper water and could not touch the bottom. She kept going under the water, but something kept popping her up to take a breath. When they got to her and pulled her out, she had not swallowed any water, and other than being scared, there was nothing wrong. Now, the glory for that goes to God, does it not? I believe, just like so many other times in my life, God sent an angel to protect Kadence. It was as if an angel lifted her up to take a breath and kept her from floating further out. Prayer is our lifeline to God, and He listens to us.

In this example, my worry or fear was that something terrible would happen at the lake. Satan often tries to steal our peace. Worry can be triggered by something seen on TV or something you read, and so forth. When we respond to these attacks with prayer instead of worry, we call on God to intervene. If you sit and worry about whatever it is, will it change anything? Do you have any power other than prayer to change it? I am confident that the answer is *no*. Only God is in control.

Faith in Trial

Rejoice in hope, be patient in tribulation,
be constant in prayer.
Romans 12:12 ESV

"I went to open the window to tell George to stop barking before he woke up all the neighbors. When I saw movement, it startled me, and I was shocked he was standing there, lurking outside our window."

White Flag of Surrender

When people who cause us distress are placed in our lives, we need to deal with the situation before moving forward. It seems when we run from our problems, they always return. It will likely be a different person or situation, but we are dealing with the same root problem. Our faith in the Lord increases throughout the trials in life, and we have to learn to stand and fight when we need to or concede when we are in the wrong. The Holy Spirit helps us discern one from the other so that we can effectively continue down the road God has laid before us. We need to learn to persevere. We may grow weary, but we must not give up.

After Link and I left trucking, we moved to Wimberley in the Texas Hill Country, about forty-five minutes southwest of Austin. Link had a job as an ironworker, and they were building the iron structures on prisons. The company owner was an old friend of Link's dad, so we lived with them for a short time. On the weekends, we hunted for our own place to rent, and we finally found something we liked. The owner of about ten acres had built six sets of free-standing duplexes. Each unit had two apartments, and they looked like little farmhouses. Each duplex unit also had a quaint front porch the neighbors shared. They were about five miles outside the town of Wimberley.

Life in the duplex was new to me. The only time I had ever lived around neighbors was the short time I had lived in Tucson after leaving trucking. It was odd to go outside and feel like people were watching me. I got the creeper vibe from the duplex owner right away, as he always seemed to be hanging around outside when I went to walk our rottweiler, George, who was in a large chain-link kennel behind our duplex. I decided I needed to give it time, but I could not believe I was already having reservations about our new residence. We had signed a six-month lease, so I would have to deal with all my issues for a while. I was beginning to believe trouble followed me wherever I went.

Like Phil Connors, Bill Murray's character in the movie "Groundhog Day," I felt like I was in a never-ending cycle, doomed to repeat the same thing over and over. I look back at times in my life and see why I felt that way. Certain things I just could not get past. I was destined to experience the same problem and repeat the same action in my life until I dealt with the issue. I was a runner, not in the healthy sense of the word, unfortunately, but I ran from difficulties. When something became taxing or there was tension, I quit. I would throw up that white flag and surrender. There was no dream enticing enough to keep me in the game when things got hard. Difficult people and situations were a part of my life from childhood, and I had never stood my ground.

According to an article on INC.com, there are fifteen reasons people seem to give up on their dreams, including fear of failure, lack of discipline, not believing in themselves, and boredom, to name a few.[12] An article on crossroadschristian.org gives the Christian perspective on why people often give up on their endeavors. In contrast, the article highlights why a Christian should not abandon their dreams. We must realize that when we are in God's will, the Enemy will attempt to stop us. These attacks can come in various ways, all meant to derail us and keep us from our calling. Satan plays on our fears and weaknesses. He never sleeps, so unfortunately, he knows how to attack effectively. If we are not on guard for the ambush, it is easy to fall victim to his schemes, and we can end up forfeiting a blessing from the Lord.[13]

As a young Christian, I was stuck in my faith. We did not go to church, and I did not study God's Word, so I was static. When faced with decisions, I had to determine what I would feed, the spirit or the flesh? Too often, I was feeding my earthly desire, and my spirit was on life support. At this point in my life, I had no concept of growing in faith through trials, so I always regarded myself as a victim of circumstance.

The owner of the property, Mr. Malroy, was a greedy person. He charged his tenants a fee for trash service but refused to pay for professional pickup. Another tenant and newfound friend, Cathy, had a truck, so he paid her a meager amount to help him dispose of the trash while he pocketed the excess. He would load the garbage in the back of her pickup, and Cathy said that before they pulled into the transfer station, he got on top of the bags and rolled around. His reasoning for this was to try to make the load look smaller so he could pay less.

Mr. Malroy came to my door on many occasions to give box smashing lessons. He would hold a box up for me to see, then place it on the floor and step on it to flatten it. It worked, I guess, because I made sure I smashed all cardboard to avoid dealing with him. As I said, he creeped me out, and I did everything in my power to steer clear of him. The Malroys had a mean Doberman that stalked me when I was walking George. He would sneak up and try to attack George or bite me. Mr. Malroy was always around but never called his dog back, so I started carrying a stick for defense.

Our duplex was the closest to Malroys' home, and our bedroom window faced their house. It was late one night after we had gone to bed, and I woke up when I heard George barking. I got up and went to open the window to tell George to stop barking before he woke up all the neighbors. When I saw movement, it startled me, and I was shocked Malroy was standing there, lurking outside our window.

"It is going to be cold tonight," he said when he realized I had seen him, "you might want to put George in the house."

Not thinking clearly and not wanting to wake up Link, I changed out of my pajamas, put a coat on, and headed out to get George. Malroy stood there watching me as I put George's leash on and walked him to our little apartment. The man never moved. He just stood there silently watching me. After that incident, I wanted out of there. We still had one month on our lease, but I no longer felt safe. Link was gone all day and occasionally at night, and I was now scared to be there alone. I was also four months pregnant and did not want the stress.

We found a new place fairly quickly, another duplex closer to town. We had paid first and last month's rent to Malroy upfront and knew we would not get that money back, but I was holding out hope we might get our deposit back. We moved into the new place, and I had someone help me clean the Malroy duplex because I had heard he checked it with a white glove. I wanted it spotless.

I was not there when Malroy inspected the duplex because I did not want to be alone with him. When I received an envelope from him, I was happy, thinking it was a refund for the deposit, and we needed the money. I was shocked when I opened it because I had received a bill for over six hundred dollars instead of a check. He had gone through that tiny apartment with his white glove and made a long list of bogus charges. It was as if I had not cleaned at all, and I was furious and frustrated. I was unsure of what to do next.

Link gave Mr. Malroy a call to discuss the charges because it was inconceivable that he felt we owed him more money. He had the last month's rent, a two-hundred-dollar pet deposit, and he was now asking for an additional six hundred dollars. He was unwilling even to discuss the bill, and the phone call ended quickly.

We found out from Cathy that there had been some drama after our departure from the duplexes. Other tenants had left in the middle of their lease but had destroyed their duplex. They put cigarettes out on the carpet, poured soda throughout the apartment, and threw their trash on the floor. When Malroy confronted them, he had a gun and pointed it at his disgruntled departing tenant, and law enforcement was involved.

Based on the new information, we concluded that Malroy was attempting to frighten us into giving him money he wasn't able to get from the other tenants. So I typed out a letter explaining that we disagreed with the charges and mailed it to him.

The response we received was further intimidation because it was a summons to Small Claims Court. I had never been to court for anything. I was so nervous, and I fretted over appearing in front of a judge. The judge, however, had dealt with Malroy on more than one occasion. Many of his tenants had received a summons from him, and we were ecstatic when the judge threw the case out. Unfortunately, our happiness over the victory was short-lived, and worry returned when a summons to County Court got delivered. We were both hoping that the county judge would also see how frivolous this was.

There are many examples of false accusations in the Bible. The ninth commandment says that you are not to bear false witness against your neighbor. When you falsely defame someone, there can be extreme judgment heaped on the accused. Jezebel first appears in the Bible in 1 Kings, and she was a hateful, bitter, spiteful woman with no regard for anyone. She was a Phoenician princess in an arranged marriage to Ahab, the king of Israel. Jezebel was a worshiper of Baal. She brought 450 prophets of Baal into the kingdom and had many of God's prophets killed.

King Ahab coveted a vineyard that belonged to a man named Naboth, who refused to sell his vineyard to the king. Ahab was so upset he sulked and refused to eat, so Jezebel promised to obtain the vineyard for him. Taking matters into her own hands, Jezebel set in motion a plan for Naboth's demise. She sent letters in the king's name to the city's nobles and elders and had them proclaim a fast. She wanted Naboth to have a seat of honor but wanted two scoundrels to sit opposite him. When the scoundrels bore false witness toward Naboth, he was taken out and stoned to death. In 2 Kings, God punishes Ahab and Jezebel, and they both die as the Lord proclaims through His prophet Elijah. King Ahab would be slain and dogs would lick his blood where they licked up Naboth's blood, and by the wall of Jezreel, Jezebel would be devoured by dogs. It happened just as God determined, and He knew it would happen that way because it was His will.[14]

When we showed up at the county courthouse, I was surprised to see the elderly couple who had lived next to us. I had not realized he would be bringing witnesses, and I had no clue what this kind couple would have to contribute to Malroy's case. They were his character witnesses, and he had them there to diminish his creep factor. He stood in the court and lied about the condition of the apartment we had vacated.

When we received the judge's decision, Link and I were relieved to see that she had sided in our favor. Malroy was being allowed to keep the security deposit, but we were not required to pay him the six hundred dollars for his bogus claim. When the official judgment came in the mail, I called the court to ask a question. When the clerk answered the phone and I told her what I was calling about, she said, "Oh yes, Mr. Malroy is here talking to the judge about this case today." I did not think much about her comment until we received a letter in the mail from the court. The judge had changed her ruling, and the letter stated that she was also adding court costs. The amount now owed was over nine hundred dollars, and regardless of our attempts to speak with the judge, she refused to see us.

I was so disheartened that I had to add this to our monthly bills, but I knew if I paid him something every month he could do nothing more. We were living from paycheck to paycheck as it was, with a baby coming. It was overwhelming. Most people buy new furniture for their homes, and when a baby is on the way, they purchase baby furniture. I was buying furniture from thrift stores. It was never what I wanted. I just tried to find something that wasn't disgusting. Everything we owned was either given to us or purchased from a thrift store. I started saving a little money every payday, and eventually, we were able to buy a washer and dryer, but we had to buy from a man who repaired appliances. When we picked them up, they were sitting in a huge dirt lot, dented and dirty, but I was excited I didn't have to go to the laundromat anymore. It's all about perspective.

There is an old English proverb that says, "It never rains, but it pours." In 1911, the Morton Salt Company developed a salt with new technology that did not clump in humid weather. Their ad agency put a twist on that proverb and came up with the slogan, "When it rains, it pours."[15] My mom said that all the time, but like most people, she used it to mean something negative, which is how I have always used it.

Well, I just thought it was raining, but it was about to start pouring at our house. Right after the judge changed her ruling, we received another gem in the mail. At this point, my spirit of perseverance was dragging itself toward some elusive finish line. I was about to wave that white flag of surrender once again.

Back in 1987, Link lived in Grand Junction, Colorado, and was driving a semi. The company had an office in Grand Junction and one in Salt Lake City, Utah. When Link had a few days off and was in Salt Lake, he would catch a small commuter plane to Grand Junction to be home.

One long weekend, he decided to fly back, so he gathered his duffle bag and a briefcase with his gun in it and headed to the Salt Lake airport. Security taped the briefcase on both ends and put a large red "Firearm" sticker on the front of the case.

In 1987, the airport in Grand Junction, Colorado, was tiny, and the person who checked your ticket also helped place baggage into the cargo hold. Passengers boarded planes by walking out on the tarmac and climbed steps to enter the aircraft. This was before the intense screening implemented due to the tragedy of 9/11.

Monday morning, Link entered the Grand Junction airport and was running late with just minutes before his flight to Salt Lake. He was carrying the case with his gun, but he had not opened it, so it was still taped up and had the sticker on the front. The ticket counter for his airline was unattended because she was on the tarmac loading luggage. Link asked an attendant of another airline, and the person directed him to the security check. Rushing up to the person at the security point, he set his bags down, asking her to check them.

Regardless of the number of times I have asked Link to dress more appropriately for airport security, he still has not listened to this day. When Link goes to the airport, he always wears his boots, hat, jeans, belt, and he has coins in his pockets. When he gets to security, he has to empty his pockets, take his belt off, and take his shoes off; he practically undresses. Well, in 1987, he didn't have to take his shoes off, but he had to empty his pockets and remove his belt, which takes time. Distracted, he did not see that the security attendant had placed his bags on the belt instead of sending them out to go in the plane's cargo hold. When it went under the scanner, the alarm sounded.

Needless to say, he missed his flight because he had to wait for local police and FBI agents to show up and question him. In the end, the authorities acknowledged the misunderstanding, and everyone there saw the humor in the situation. Link had to wait for a flight the following day, but other than that, all agents agreed there was no violation.

I was clueless about this incident until a letter came in the mail from the Federal Aviation Administration. It was a bill for over $2,500, a violation for attempting to board an aircraft with a firearm. I was beyond frustrated, but I eventually had to get over the anger and try to fix the situation. Calling the FAA left both of us feeling defeated because they just wanted the money, and in their minds, that was the only resolution. Therefore, the FBI was my only alternative. When I spoke to an agent from the FBI office in Grand Junction, they were able to look the case up and verify that there had been no charge made, and it was closed. Since the agent had retired, I would have to contact the main office for a copy of the report. The only insight the FBI agent could give me on the bill was that the statute of limitations was about to run out, and it could be an attempt to see if we would pay it. In other words, it came across someone's desk, and instead of looking into the validity of the violation, they just sent a bill.

After the initial call that Link made to the FAA, they knew they had the correct address, and they increased the intimidation tactics, threatening stiffer fines and jail time. The collection calls were constant, and I was afraid to answer my phone. I contacted the main FBI office and requested a copy of the report, but found it could take months to receive.

After about six months of nonstop harassment, the intimidation finally stopped. We assumed the statute of limitations had run out, and they abandoned their attempt. I found it unsettling that a mistake made by an FAA employee would cause us such grief, and they were unapologetic about their tactics. Our attempts to get them to contact the FBI fell on deaf ears. People in positions of power can be your best ally or your worst enemy, depending on how willing they are to help.

They didn't succeed in making us pay the fine, but that does not mean their harassment and intimidation did not have a lasting effect on us. The anxiety lingered for years as we worried whether they might contact us again. I hated being afraid to answer my phone.

Afterthought

Looking back on this time, I realize how young and clueless we were. We went into battle unarmed—without God's Word—and since we lacked faith for victory, we failed to prevail. We submitted to harassment and did not pursue justice. We lacked the trust to believe that God would fight our battle and the determination to win the war. We should have gone boldly forward without fear, but we chose to give up. We were intimidated, and we allowed fear to cripple us.

Intimidation can be a powerful tool, and when used by those in positions of authority, it can immobilize someone. In 2019, imposter scams were the number one complaint made to the Federal Trade Commission, and the reported loss from victims was over $667 million.[16] Imposters claiming to be calling from the Social Security office was the top scam reported. Those scammers threatened increased fines and even imprisonment, so intimidation works.

I still have no idea what Mr. Malroy said to the judge that made her change her verdict. There are shady deals made every day because we live in a fallen world, and Satan prowls around like a lion looking for people he can devour (1 Peter 5:8). When dealing with the unsaved, we must remember that they lack conviction. In other words, they do not play by our rules.

In the case of the intimidation from the FAA, I am thankful that the limitation ran out because I have been waiting twenty-eight years for that FBI report.

Second Corinthians 10:4 says that the weapons we possess for warfare in Christ have divine power to destroy strongholds. With faith and prayer, we can move mountains. God would have interceded on our behalf, but we did not ask, so we did not receive His help. He never promised that we would have a life free of turmoil but to expect trouble. God wants us to rely on Him because our lack of ability highlights His power, and He is the one who deserves the glory.

Faith Lesson: God wants us to persevere. Quitting is taking the easy way out and not aligning with God's will. It is imperative to ask the Lord for help because we cannot expect to receive something we do not pray for.

Ranch Talk

The homely, flea-bitten, gray gelding, Banjo, was the first horse that I did not have to share with my sister because I had purchased him with my own money.

He was as mean as he was ugly, and the day we unloaded him into the corral, I took some grain to feed to him. I was so excited and just knew this relationship was going to be the fantasy portrayed in books. I lovingly poured the grain in his feeder, stroking his shoulder and speaking kindly to him, but as I turned to walk away, he kicked me square in the butt, which catapulted me across the pen and head-first into another feeder.

I placed my hope, trust, and faith in that gray nag and he betrayed me. His betrayal did not stop with this incident because we ended up having a long relationship based on his treachery. He was counterfeit and never missed an opportunity to cheat me. I rode him bareback most of the time, and he would try to turn out from underneath me frequently. We would be loping along in the pasture headed one way around a bush, and at the last second, he would turn the opposite direction. I believe this may be the only area in my young life that I did not give up easily on an attempt to love this horse. I considered him a friend, but like others in my life, he was in the enemy's camp.

There is only One that will never forsake us, and that is God. As human beings, we often act like that gray nag because God heaps love and mercy on us, and we are the ones who betray Him. The Lord is like the parent in the grandstands rooting for us, not wanting us to quit, desiring us to achieve the glory that comes at the end. We are akin to the child on the field who cannot see any possibility of victory, and in frustration, gives up so close to triumph. Like that child who accuses the parent of his failure, we blame God for our failures.

Believer, you must fight to the end, because the Lord wants you to be victorious, and if you are living inside His will, He does fight for you.

Prayer

Lord, I come before You and humbly ask for Your protection and guidance in my life. I pray, heavenly Father, for the courage to face my adversaries and to persevere so I will not grow weary and give up. I do not want to be dense like a horse or mule that must be controlled with a bridle and bit, and I ask for Your counsel, Lord. Please help me understand and discern Your Word and be victorious in fighting the good fight. In Jesus' name I pray, amen.

Study

There can be beauty from the ashes. A person's perspective is the key to their attitude on life. I once read an article in *Forbes* magazine that talked about how expectations of good things happening bears positive results; in contrast, negative expectations can immobilize you.[17] So if you believe that only bad things happen, you tend to be afraid even to attempt anything, and you remain static.

A motivational speaker named Les Brown said, "Shoot for the moon and if you miss you will still be among the stars."[18] So we need to dream big and have a positive attitude. As Christians, we should expect the best in life, because God is faithful when we seek His will. If what we ask is not God's will, we must trust that He is protecting us. If you were catching a flight to take a dream vacation, and you prayed for God's protection and will, would you be upset if you missed your flight? Most people would say yes. Would you still be mad if you found out that the plane you missed had crashed? It's all about perspective and the glasses we look through. None of us know all of the tragedies that God has kept us from enduring.

William Carey was a missionary at the end of the eighteenth century. In a very influential sermon, Carey said, "Ask great things of God; attempt great things for God."[19] So if you are in God's will, expect the best knowing that God wants the best for us. Don't be afraid to ask God, because He wants us to come to Him with our requests. I have learned to ask without fear, and I know that if I don't get what I ask for, it would not have been a blessing. God's will should be your desire.

Look up John 15:7 and write it down. _____
_____
_____

Write down the things you believe are needed and pray daily for God's guidance and will in that area. Trust that God is doing what is best for you, even if it is not what you want. You do not know when an unanswered prayer is God protecting you. I have given you an example of what I should have prayed over our situation above.

I Come Before You Lord to Pray Over	I Humbly Ask
Our upcoming court appearance	To be absolved from this false claim

Now pray over your problems.

I pray for your guidance and will in all areas of my life, Lord, but especially concerning _____.
I cast off doubt that the Enemy wants to whisper in my ear, choosing to believe Your promise instead. I humbly ask _____
_____. I know that You see all things, Lord, and that You are in control of everything. You know what is best for me, and You love and protect me. I trust that You will work all things for my good, heavenly Father. In Jesus' name I pray, amen.

Shielded in Faith

But you, O Lord, are a shield around me;
you are my glory, the one who holds my head high.
Psalm 3:3 NLT

"That is the type of person who would come back to slit the family's throats and burn the house down." Link said, "I just told him to go ahead and take it."

Unforeseen Dangers

God is the perfect loving Father. Like babies, we totter toward an elusive "happiness" and go about our daily lives, thinking we are in control of everything. But the Lord determines our steps and works in our life, patiently sheltering us under His wings. He intervenes daily to protect us from situations that could derail or destroy us, and if we will humbly turn to Him when we stumble, He is faithful to both shield us and restore us.

In September of 1992, after thirty-six hours of labor, our daughter Taylor came into our lives. She was big, weighing 9 pounds 3 ounces, and she was a healthy, happy baby girl. Before she was born, my mom rode the Amtrak to San Marcos, Texas, the little town southeast of Wimberley, and I was so relieved to have her there to help me. She stayed for two weeks, and I was sad the day we took her back to the Amtrak station, and she headed home. Her leaving reminded me of my loneliness and isolation. I was missing my family.

In the summer of 1994, I told Link I was ready to move back to Arizona. He was committed to finishing a prison job close to his dad's house in Alto, Texas, so he moved in with them, and Taylor and I headed west, back to Arizona. One of Link's grandmas was kind enough to let us live in her apartment, and when he finished the prison job, Link followed. He tried to make a living around the area for a while, but in 1996, Link headed back to Texas. Our friends, Cathy and Gill, had started a business around Corpus Christi welding on oil rigs, and Link went to work for them.

Life was not easy, but God has a way of placing us where He wants us. At this time, I was not consciously seeking to discover what God's purpose was for my life, but He was still working. Unexpectedly, my cousin, who had played a part in introducing me to Link, called and asked if I would be interested in a place closer to my parents. Her father-in-law, Ron, and her husband, Peter, were ranchers who helped my dad during spring and fall works, so I had known them most of my life. There was a ranch that Ron leased with a house that needed a tenant. I was not going to have to pay rent or utilities, so I jumped at the opportunity. The downside was that it was close to the Mexico border, and drug smugglers and human traffickers regularly traveled by this place. Houses that sat empty were typically broken into and destroyed because they would use them as a campsite and build fires in the middle of the floor.

When I was in college, three ladies from across the border were employed where I worked, and they would come from Mexico daily.

During that time, which was in the late eighties, there were horrible murders linked to the drug cartel in Mexico, and these ladies brought Mexico newspapers across that showed the graphic details.[20] I will never forget the horror of those pictures.

In 1990, federal agents discovered a tunnel exposing an elaborate scheme constructed to move drugs across the border undetected. It was an intricate design, which started with a pool table on hydraulics in a luxury home in Mexico. The pool table in the house lifted off the floor to provide access to a 270-foot underground tunnel. The tunnel had lighting and elaborate passageways and surfaced inside a warehouse across the border in America. Estimated at the cost of over one million dollars to engineer, this was the first of many tunnels to come. Between 1990 and 2013, authorities found over 140 more underground trafficking passageways along the California and Arizona border. However, over 60 percent of the tunnels discovered were in Arizona, though none were as elaborate as the first.[21]

Human smuggling and drug trafficking in this area have steadily increased over the years, and unfortunately, those who pay for passage experience many horrors. Traffickers are ruthless, and these mafia cartels are in it just for the money. Ranchers in these areas know firsthand the immorality surrounding human smugglers; after all, it is a trade run by evil. Too often, people who have paid the coyotes (those who smuggle immigrants into the US) to bring them across are run over and left, or they die of thirst, starvation, or worse. An estimated 60 percent of female migrants experience sexual assault. Cartels have made it known that they like trafficking people because, unlike drugs, they can sell them repeatedly until "they are too broken to be used anymore."[22] It is a horrible thought but an unfortunate reality in a domain ruled by Satan.

The evil coming across the border chooses the path of least resistance, which places ranchers on the front lines because smugglers travel across their land.[23] I grew up in this reality and decided to move back to the battlefield; only now, I would be solely responsible for protecting our daughter. The home we were moving to sat close to a dirt road that was a cut off to a larger border town. It was unpoliced and a popular route for smugglers. There was one close neighbor about a quarter of a mile away.

The ranch house was an old army barracks that had been moved and set on a concrete foundation and was by no means my dream home. It was a small single-story house with three bedrooms and one bathroom. It was old, the floor had worn linoleum, and the appliances were outdated. It had one gas heater and a swamp cooler in the living room to heat and cool the whole house, but it was free. I cleaned before Taylor and I moved in, and when the day came, it was just the two of us, our rottweiler, George, and a few horses.

It was nice being back on a ranch and among old family and friends, but the nights could be rather daunting, and when darkness fell, I made sure we were always locked inside. We not only had a border to the south, but there was a camp for troubled teens to the north of this place. There was no phone landline, but I did have a cellular bag phone, so I at least had a lifeline. It was reassuring that a Highway Patrol officer and his family rented the house across the road, and I chose to stay oblivious to the outside world at night.

It is easy for me to close my eyes to things that go on around me because I tend to keep to myself and stay out of others' affairs. Link does not, and he likes to know what is going on around him, so he befriended the officer across the road when he was home for a few days. The officer informed him that he would not want to know what travels by our homes daily. Since the cartel continuously trafficked drugs and people through the area, it was best not to get involved.

With Link working back in Texas, we did not see him often. He was typically gone two or three months and would come home for about a week. Since Taylor was so young, he missed most of her milestones growing up. I felt like her supervisor, principal, teacher, and security guard all in one. I was a married, single parent, but thankful to have people I had known most all my life so close to me now. Taylor started calling Ron, Grandpa Ron, and his wife, Grandma May. Unfortunately, Ron was fighting cancer, and I tried hard not to place my problems on his shoulders but he was always worried about us.

It was difficult not having Link home, and with little money and living so far from town, I had to learn to do most everything myself. I changed flat tires on my pickup, which always seemed to be the inside dual tire. I fed and doctored animals, repaired fences, and disciplined a young girl who did not seem to like me very much. I became a stressed and angry person, and like a pressure cooker, I vented when I became overwhelmed. I tended to romanticize events in my head, but I would ruin experiences for Taylor because I had no patience when they didn't turn out as planned.

The first day of school should be memorable with new clothes, shoes, school supplies, and of course, the "first day of school" picture. We were running late that morning, and the more I attempted to rush, the slower Taylor became. I practically pushed her out the front door to the pickup, my frustration increasing with each step. Backing up, I turned the truck around, put it in gear, and realized I had forgotten the camera. I threw the pickup into neutral, pushed the emergency brake, and ran back into the house to grab the camera. The pressure was building as I unlocked the front door, found the camera, and ran back to the pickup. Wanting to scream now, I put the vehicle in gear and sped toward the gate at the cattleguard. We still had to unlock the chain on the gate, open it, and then close and relock it before we drove the nine miles of dirt road to the school.

I practically slid to a stop in my haste, and Taylor got out and sauntered toward the gate, which made my blood boil. I grabbed the camera and stepped out of the pickup to take her picture. She was mad because when I got stressed out, I would typically yell a lot, and because she did not seem to care if she was late, I was becoming increasingly angry. With the camera in hand, I started to take the picture and yelled, "Smile!" When she gave me the "I-am-going-to-force-a-stupid-smile" pose, the pot boiled over. I don't remember ever spanking Taylor, but I sure shouted a lot, as if "hurry" worked better at an extreme volume. In the aftermath, I felt like the ultimate failure.

I was weary of bearing the sole responsibility of raising our daughter and being alone. So, I was thankful when Link also became tired of being away, and we decided he should move back to Arizona. Having him home was bittersweet because he did not make as much money. It was always feast or famine, and generally, it was famine.

I wanted him there with us, but we inevitably got further and further behind on bills. So eventually, he would have to leave home for decent pay. I just tried to enjoy the times he was home and the security of him being there.

One day, on our way to town, we noticed an old Ford Bronco broken down in front of a wire gate. Two weeks later, the Bronco still sat in the same place, so we stopped to look it over. The inside was bare because the owner had removed all seats except the passenger and driver seats. It was dirty, and it stunk because there were backpacks with rotting food in them. It was a typical smuggling vehicle. We left it alone, believing they would be back to pick it up. However, another week passed, and there it sat, unmoved, still blocking a gate. Eventually, Link and Peter towed it to our barn, and after a couple more months, we filed for an abandoned title to use it for parts.

Months after filing the paperwork, I was returning from town. As I pulled up to our gate, a man and woman were standing in front of the cattleguard. She was laughing and flirting with him, but when I pulled up, their faces became solemn. I put my pickup in park and stepped out to unlock and open the gate. They were both Hispanic, impeccably dressed, and the man was quite a bit older than his girlfriend. I wasn't sure what to expect, but as I walked to the gate, they approached me. "Can I help you?" I was not overly friendly.

The woman is the one who spoke. "That is our Bronco," she said. "We were out here four-wheeling, and it broke down."

I knew that was a lie because I did not believe the two standing in front of me would be driving a vehicle in that condition, especially when I looked at the luxury vehicle parked on the side of the road.

"You need to come back and talk to my husband about that," I said, annoyed that they had waited so long to come to get it.

The man spoke to her in Spanish, and she asked, "What time will that be?"

"He will be home around three." I swung the gate open and got back in my pickup. When I got out to close the gate, they walked to their car, and I knew the man was not happy, but I did not care.

I called Link and told him what had happened, and that they would most likely be there when he got home. He was as annoyed as I was and we decided to charge them a storage fee. Since we had towed it to our yard, they had avoided impound and auction of the vehicle.

I did not think much more about it, but I looked out the window when it was close to three. The cattleguard with the locked gate was about three hundred yards from the house, so I could see they were standing there, waiting.

When Link pulled up, I saw them talking, and then he opened the gate, and they pulled in behind him. The couple drove out to the Bronco, and Link parked and came into the house.

I was looking at him when he walked in, curious about what they had said. Link was uneasy. "That dude is evil," he said. "He has to be a drug lord and looked at me like he wanted to kill me." He was gathering some things up, getting ready to head back outside. "That is the type of person who would come back to slit the family's throats and burn the house down," Link said. "I just told him to go ahead and take it."

He walked out, and I watched him go through the gate and towards the group of people. I was nervous now. "Please help us, God," I uttered the plea softly, not wanting to alarm Taylor.

The man had several other men there to help him, and they had the vehicle chained to a pickup and were towing it away from the barn. Link said the steering wheel had come loose from the column, and when he walked up, the man was holding it in his hands. Link and Peter had removed it when they towed the vehicle in, so Link quickly fixed it. When they were ready to leave, the man pulled a baseball-sized wad of one-hundred-dollar bills out of his pocket and asked how much he owed us.

Just wanting him to leave, Link replied, "No, you don't owe me anything. I am happy you found it." Link said he flaked off two of the bills and insisted he take them. We were both happy to see them driving off and thankful he was leaving satisfied. Evil people do horrible things when they are angry.

I feel that people who operate in such an evil business are most likely demon possessed. It is inconceivable how someone could be so hard-hearted toward the suffering of other human beings. The Bible says that demons must inhabit a body or they have no rest or evil power. Matthew 12:43–44 (NKJV) says, "When an unclean spirit goes out of a man, he goes through dry places, seeking rest, and finds none. Then he says, 'I will return to my house from which I came.' And when he comes, he finds *it* empty, swept, and put in order." The New American Standard Bible uses the term "unoccupied," which tells us that the demon searches for dwellings or bodies that have a "vacancy sign." It is also possible for many demons to possess a nonbeliever at the same time. Matthew 12:45 (NLT) says, "Then the spirit finds seven other spirits more evil than itself, and they all enter the person and live there. And so that person is worse off than before."

The Bible informs us that demon possession is a reality, and that fact gives validity to inherent evil. When someone commits incredibly heinous acts and is indifferent to suffering, it seems plausible that something demonic likely inhabits them. If there are varying degrees of evil amongst demons, and many can indwell a person simultaneously, then that person's depraved actions have no bounds.

Although we should not be obsessed about the topic of evil, it is essential to understand that we do have a spiritual world surrounding us. In it, there are both heavenly angels and fallen angels, and spiritual warfare takes place continuously.[24] Born-again believers, however, have protection around them, and our greatest weapon is prayer. With prayer, we invoke God's immense power, and He will intervene to keep us safe and fulfill His plan. It doesn't take an elaborate prayer, just humbly calling on His name and trusting in Him. We need to realize and acknowledge that we are powerless to fight the Enemy alone.

Link listened as God spoke that day and revealed the evil to him, so with kindness and humility, he was able to defuse the situation. Proverbs 15:1 says it is a kind word that defuses a person's anger. I stirred the wrath, and God had brought Link home so that he would be there to douse it. Evil cannot stand against God; it shrinks from the light.

The Bible reminds us repeatedly not to be afraid. We have to stand on God's promises and remember that He strategically positions people and controls situations for our benefit and protection. He had brought Link home from Texas to handle this, and He revealed the danger to him. That man showed his unwillingness to deal with me by speaking through his girlfriend; however, he had no problem speaking English to Link. I do not doubt that God shielded us from the Enemy that day.

When living in God's will, it is imperative to remember that we have an Enemy who relentlessly strives to destroy or disrupt God's plan for us. We must continue the course undaunted because God will provide a shield of protection around us.

Afterthought

I have to say that I realize America's southern border is a touchy subject for many people. Ignoring this, however, does nothing but perpetuate the harm done to the men, women, and children who are subjected to this evil every day. Satan is ruling this planet right now, and no one needs to look very hard to realize that so many lost people are doing his bidding.

I have heard people mistakenly claim that the Bible says, "Money is the root of all evil." That is not accurate because 1 Timothy 6:10 (ESV) states, "For the love of money is a root of all kinds of evil." Therefore, it is not money, but rather the love of money. When a person will do absolutely anything for money, they have sold their soul to the devil. A person who is willing to sell someone until they are "too broken to be used any more" is indwelt by evil.[25]

Since I was uncivil to that man and his girlfriend the day they came about the vehicle, they could have retaliated in numerous ways. It is a huge personal offense to someone like this man to be slighted and disrespected, especially by a woman. Thankfully, God worked through Link, and he doused the anger and removed any motivation he may have had for revenge. The Holy Spirit is our guide, but we must be willing to listen. If we act as unruly school children and boldly do as we please with no regard to our inner guidance, then we are subject to the consequences. When we realize we are powerless over our circumstances, we can be humble in every situation and pray knowing that the Lord has all power. God can use anyone or anything to change an outcome. Our only shield against evil is Him, and He can work all things for good. However, we must also remember that God will not always shield us from something that will ultimately make us stronger.

In the movie *The Curious Case of Benjamin Button*, there is a scene where the lead heroine, Daisy, an accomplished ballerina, is struck by a taxi. The accident is a life-altering, career-ending tragedy. The narration goes through a series of events that ultimately placed Daisy in the path of that vehicle. It shows how crucial timing is, and how one minor event could change an outcome because it changes the situation. An example from the movie is a woman who forgot her coat and went back for it, which delayed her departure by a few minutes. If she had not forgotten the item, the taxi would have passed by before Daisy crossed the street, and it would not have struck her. The scenario deals with time, but this concept can apply to any situation, be it a word spoken, an action taken, or any other behavior that ultimately changes an outcome.

The critical thing to remember is that God controls everything, including our schedule and interactions. There are catastrophes we often unknowingly avoid due to His intercession. When traffic slows me down, I try to remind myself that it could be because God is keeping me from something. When I put possible outcomes into perspective, I know I would prefer to make it to my destination a few minutes late than not at all because of an accident.

I remember parking at a store in a sketchy area, and when I walked in, I noticed a guy hanging around the front. There was no one else around, and I took note of him because he seemed unsettled and nervous. I went in, and as I was shopping, I forgot about him. I checked out, and as soon as I stepped out the front door, I saw him again, and he silently fell in behind me as I walked to my car. I felt very threatened as he seemed to get closer to me, but I didn't want to look over my shoulder to see where he was. I said a silent prayer, asking for protection, and almost instantly after the prayer, he brushed past me, quickly walking away. He had been so close to me that he almost bumped into me as he went by. When I looked up, I saw a couple of men and their girlfriends who had just stepped out of their pickup and were walking in my direction.

Now you may see this as just a coincidence, but I genuinely believe that if they had not stepped out of their vehicle at that precise second, he would have robbed me or worse. When our first thought or reaction is to turn to God and pray, He is faithful to shield us, or He allows it in order to perfect us.

Faith Lesson: God can use a person's humility, words, and actions to shield us from danger. Turning to God should always be our first thought. We need to ask for His help in every situation.

Ranch Talk

There was a time when I was helping Grandpa Ron's son, Peter, gather cattle. I started the day annoyed because he had teenagers who wanted to sleep in, and they did not want to leave the house until 10:00 a.m. Summer in Arizona is already blazing hot at that time. Taylor was with us that morning, riding her horse Coffee Pot, and everything was going wrong. One of the dogs got overheated and was not doing well, the cattle we were gathering were trashy, and issues kept mounting as the morning dragged on. We were gathering in a pasture riddled with prairie dog burrows. I saw Peter loping towards me, but his horse stepped in a hole and flipped forward. It looked like he fell right on Peter. I told Taylor to stay put, and I loped to him to make sure he was okay.

Peter and the horse were getting up when I got close, but Taylor, in a reasonably calm voice, started saying, "Mom. . . Mom." At this point, my inner stress was building, especially since I started the day annoyed. Taylor's tone was more panicked when she repeated, "Mom. . . Mom!"

Exasperated and thinking she was just worried about being alone, I shouted, "Hang on, Taylor, I will be there in a minute!" Peter and his horse got up unharmed, and as he got on his horse, I turned to ride back toward Taylor. It did not take long to see why she was calling for me. Taylor had bees crawling all over her, and they were practically covering her shirt, face, and cap. It looked like a scene from a bad horror movie. Frightened, I kicked my horse up, Peter right behind me, and when I reached her, I grabbed her hat and flung it to the ground. Peter pulled her off the horse, knocking bees off, and put her on my horse in front of me. We ran out of the bees.

Each of us was stung several times, but thankfully, neither of us was allergic. Grandpa Ron had just happened to pull up to the fence in his pickup, and I handed her to him. Struck with guilt, I fought back the tears. Seeing my child covered in bees was one of the most frightening things I had experienced with my children . . . well, at this point in my life anyway.

Like most people, I can look back at things that happened in my past and see how the outcome could have been tragically different. Many attribute this to being "lucky," and they do not see God's intercession, shielding, and grace. I understand why the unsaved would use the term "lucky," but if we are believers and genuinely trust the Bible, how can we possibly use that term? Since God is our faithful shelter from every storm, then the praise is His, and we must give Him the glory. The Lord deserves exaltation and expects us to be thankful and glorify Him.

Prayer

Heavenly Father, I give You the glory. I will praise Your name, Lord, and humbly ask for Your continued protection and intervention in my life. I know You are in control of all things, Father, and that You shield me from evil and shelter me from the raging storm. I thank You, Lord, for I see the tribulation You have protected me from, and I acknowledge that You have rescued me from many trials, many I am unaware of. You are my Shield and my Savior, Father. I thank You and will forever praise Your name. In Jesus' name I pray, amen.

Study

Give thanks to the Lord! Everything we have is from God, and we need to acknowledge that and give the glory to Him.

Psalm 121:1–2 (ESV) says, "I lift up my eyes to the hills. From where does my help come? My help comes from the Lord, who made heaven and earth."

Look up and write out the last two verses of Psalm 121, verses 7–8.

_____

_____

_____

_____

_____

Now take some time to think, making sure you are in a quiet place where you will not be interrupted. Put some thought into this question.

What things in your life are you thankful for? _____

_____

_____

_____

Now think back on your life and the things you have experienced, good or bad. List times in your life that God interceded on your behalf. It could be an accident you were spared from or survived, a person who spoke on your behalf, and so forth.

1. _____
2. _____
3. _____
4. _____
5. _____

Acknowledge the blessings God has placed on your life. Real joy comes from the appreciation of things given to us by the Lord. Until we change the lenses of the glasses we look through, we cannot change our perspective on life.

Misplaced Faith

"Their land is full of idols; the people worship things
they have made with their own hands."
Isaiah 2:8 NLT

"I was unsure of what was about to transpire. I had no idea how my life would change, no clue how the cry of that baby girl, the cry that set the hospital staff in motion, would launch us on a journey for which we were both ill-prepared."

Season of Change

There are times in our lives when things do not work out as we planned, days when we are disappointed, and we look up and wonder, "Where are you, Lord?" We clutch tightly to idols we have built for ourselves, thinking they will help us, but as children of God, we must remember to look up. Help doesn't come from ourselves but from the One who keeps us (Psalm 121). When we misplace faith in earthly things, tribulation comes so those idols will be broken and cast down. God is the only real, sustainable resource because the worldly things we bow down to are fleeting and unreliable.

Link and I had a habit of going forth boldly, determining our own path without seeking God's will. In our lives, God was the book on the shelf. We brought Him out in times of trouble, but when the seas were calm, we left Him there to gather dust. We should have realized at this point that the Lord was tearing down an idol we kept seeking. We were chasing money, not God. I kept thinking that when we had enough money saved up, we would be secure, and then nothing would be able to shake us. However, in the earthquake to come, our world would be turned upside down.

God was launching us on a treacherous journey, and if I could have seen the road that lay ahead, I would have cowered in fear. Like the Israelites who wandered in the wilderness, we would stumble in the desert for many years as we continued to cling to idols instead of God.

Link hired on with a new company and was installing the boiler rooms in hydroponic greenhouses. These were massive structures, and some of them covered forty acres or more. At first, since it was only an hour away from home, he was commuting every day. The money was great, and we finally had health insurance.

Taylor and I stayed busy with daily life. We attended the church that my oldest sister and her in-laws attended, and I volunteered at Awana (a children's ministry program) on Wednesday nights. Taylor was a great kid, and we developed a close bond because we were alone most of the time. Oh, we had our issues, but she kept me sane. In the summer of 1998, we found out we were going to have another baby. There was much to be thankful for, but we still had our trials.

Grandpa Ron had been battling cancer for an extensive period, and it was the year my mom started that battle as well. Mom was one of the toughest women I knew, and she never complained. Through the turmoil of battling this deadly enemy, my mom fought bravely and, thankfully, entered remission.

At the beginning of 1999, Grandpa Ron lost his war with cancer. Our hearts broke over the tremendous loss, and I was distressed as I got in my pickup to go and get Link for the funeral. He was working in a town five hours from us and had no other way home. My heart was heavy, and alone in the cab of my pickup, I drove and cried as I thought about the man we had lost.

After Ron's funeral, things continued on a downhill slide. Before Link could get back to work, the company collapsed. The owner had lived rather extravagantly, and it had finally caught up with him. Almost overnight, without warning to any of his employees, he filed bankruptcy and closed his doors. I couldn't see how things could get any worse. I was terrified, but we decided to self-pay the six hundred dollars for our health insurance, even though Link's income was gone. Our world was beginning to quake, and the money idol I had placed prominently on the shelf was teetering, preparing to topple and shatter into pieces.

This baby was coming regardless of our financial circumstances, and a week later, I sat at my next doctor's appointment. I picked up a magazine in the waiting room and flipped through the pages. A story caught my eye. It was a heart-wrenching story about a young mother and the delivery of her first child. After a difficult labor and delivery, they had removed the baby from the room but assured her everything was fine. Her husband reassured her by insisting that the hospital staff was being cautious, but the baby was fine.

Unbeknownst to the mother, however, the baby's limbs had not fully formed in the womb. After several hours of placating the mother, her husband had to tell her the truth. I put the magazine down and considered the situation for a minute. It would have been easier if the mother would have known right away, I thought, if the husband had not hidden the information from her. It would be difficult, regardless, and something that would change a person's life forever. I brushed off the uneasy feeling. I had always been healthy, and this pregnancy had been easy, without issues or concerns.

Hearing my name, I got up and walked back for my appointment. After the doctor examined me, he said, "I am estimating the baby's size at around four pounds." He looked at my chart and continued, "This says your first baby weighed over nine pounds. Is that accurate?" He looked up from the paper, waiting for my response.

"She weighed nine pounds, three ounces," I said.

"I am worried about the dramatic difference in the size of your first baby and this one," he said, "I want to send you for an ultrasound next week, and we will go from there."

After explaining to him the difference in the amount of weight I had gained with my first pregnancy and this one, he assured me it was just a precaution. I wasn't worried and left the office excited to find out if we would have a boy or a girl. A week later, Link and I walked in for our first ultrasound undaunted. We were a bit disappointed to find out we were having another girl, but we were still unconcerned about her size.

In the next couple of days, I received a call from the doctor's office. He was sending me to get another ultrasound in a larger city. The physician's assistant said, "If the specialist wants to deliver her, Dr. Lindel said you need to consent to that."

A week later, when Link and I walked into the doctor's office in Tucson, two hours from our home, we were beginning to feel uneasy. We sat silently in the waiting room until they finally called us back.

I laid on the examining table as the sonographer squirted the jelly on my stomach and quietly began the procedure. The process was unnerving as the tech moved the transducer over my stomach. The tech would click on an area, quickly jot down information, and then move to the next spot. The whole situation was maddening as she silently worked—click, jot, repeat. The tech was a closed book, and we could not obtain any information from her even though Link was persistent. Her responses to his questions came in nods and pursed lips as she attempted to disregard his probing.

"She cannot give us that information," I said. "Quit asking her questions." I was as anxious and annoyed as he was but knew the tech was in a difficult position.

When the test was complete, she wiped off some of the gel and handed me paper towels to finish the job. "You can get dressed and go to the waiting room until the doctor is ready," she said as she exited.

We sat in the waiting room and time seemed to stop. I closed my eyes and attempted to calm my nerves, but Link was agitated. "I wish someone would just tell us something," he said, unable to hide his irritation.

Seconds later, the doctor walked out and sat in a chair in front of us. He leaned forward, placing his elbows on his knees and looking at each of us. He was somber as he bluntly stated, "I do have concerns," he sighed, "the amniotic fluid is abnormally high, which indicates a problem."

"So, what exactly does that mean?" Link asked.

Dr. Patel looked at Link and plainly stated, "This baby is going to have a congenital disability such as Down syndrome, spina bifida, cerebral palsy, or various other issues." His demeanor indicated that, for him, delivering such news was routine. "We won't know until she is delivered," he continued, "and we need to deliver her now."

We were expecting something akin to the baby being in distress or holding out as long as possible so she could grow but nothing like a potential disability. We were unprepared for such heartbreaking news, and we sat in shock and disbelief. A child with special needs was not in my plan, but God doesn't make mistakes. I should have remembered that the Lord works all things for the good of those who love Him, as Romans 8:28 promises, but I didn't. There were trials and heartbreak ahead, but also tremendous blessings and joy.

In the situation we were in, choosing abortion never crossed our minds and would not have been an option. Late-term abortion is horrific, and I think that any doctor who advocates for an abortion in the late stages of development is abhorrent. People need to realize that the doctor is dismembering a viable baby who feels pain. These babies receive nothing to alleviate their suffering.[26]

We live in a society that praises "perfection" while ridiculing those who fall short of that perceived mark. Unfortunately, the fear of judgment is a driving force behind many abortions, especially when a possible disability is involved.

Between 1998 and 2011, a staggering 67 percent of pregnancies with babies prenatally diagnosed with Down syndrome ended in abortion due to societal bias.[27] The societal stigma influences many doctors and much of the general public to advocate for the termination of babies deemed imperfect. It is disturbing to think that a child prenatally diagnosed with a disability is seen as unworthy of life. The realization that many decide on abortion based on the results of one test is even more distressing.[28] What if that one test was inaccurate? Many who choose abortion will live with feelings of profound loss for years or even a lifetime after that decision.[29]

The pro-choice movement would have us believe that a mother carries a blob of fetal tissue in her womb. The pro-life movement wants us to see that tissue as a tiny human being. How does God view it? Jeremiah 1:5 (NLT) says, "I knew you before I formed you in your mother's womb. Before you were born I set you apart." God views that "blob of tissue" as a baby He formed, and He has a plan for that human being. The pro-choice movement has been relatively successful in removing emotion from the equation. Lacking emotional attachment and viewing the fetus as a "blob" makes it easier to terminate a pregnancy. However, studies show that most pregnant mothers have an unknown emotional attachment to the fetus, even in the early stages of pregnancy. Many women ache for their lost child for years after the procedure. A 2019 article from The Daily Caller features stories from women who regret abortion.[30] The sad reality is that one encouraging word could have changed their decision, because the fear of judgment drives many women to that choice.

When the Pharisees brought the woman caught in adultery to Jesus for judgment, they were attempting to trap Him. In their minds, the only two decisions He could make would ensnare Him and expose Him as a fraud. The Pharisees were utterly unprepared when Jesus said, "He who is without sin among you, let him throw a stone at her first" (John 8:7 NKJV).

As recorded in the Bible, every person in the crowd left until just Jesus and the woman remained. Jesus was the only person there without sin, the only one who could have cast a stone. However, Jesus did not come to condemn the world but to save it (John 3:17). It is human nature to attempt to look past that plank in our eye to try to remove that speck out of someone else's eye. Matthew 7 and Luke 6 both record Jesus' command that we must first address our sin before trying to help another. When we can approach someone with love and understanding, then we can make a difference.

Fear of judgment and the unknown made my heart race. I felt numb as my mind switched to autopilot. They rushed us into labor and delivery at the hospital, and the process was immediately set in motion. Everything was happening so fast, and I had no time to process the situation mentally. I was in a bed with an IV in my arm, induction started, and we waited. Once the initial rush had passed, I laid in my room with ample time to think. Link was meeting up with my oldest sister and Mom, who volunteered to get Taylor, so I was alone. The only noise came from the machines, and I could hear the rapid heartbeat of the tiny girl in my womb.

The afternoon dragged on. Link was back, but we didn't have much to say to each other, so the room was quiet. Periodically, a specialist walked in, each with their idea of why we were in our current predicament.

As we sat in silence, another specialist walked through the door. She introduced herself and said, "One possibility we may be facing is that the baby's esophagus could have fused to her trachea." She looked at us expecting a response but was met with blank stares, so she continued. "We will need to run a tube down her throat immediately after delivery to see if that is what we are dealing with." Her statement was blunt, her demeanor stiff, and her face expressionless.

"What happens if that is the case?" Link asked.

Her face softened a little, "We will take her in for immediate surgery," she said. Then looking at each of us, she uttered, "Okay?" Turning, she walked out of the room. We looked at each other but had nothing to say. The whirlwind of information was overwhelming, and we had not prepared for any of this.

As the afternoon turned into evening, I could see the light fading from the window above the couch. I had received a phone call from a friend and responded without processing her words. With the epidural, I was feeling no physical pain, but the emotional pain was intense. The evening turned to night, and other than the machines and the occasional nurse, the room remained quiet.

The day's conversations were running through my mind as I laid on the hard bed. The beeping of the monitor was rhythmic but subdued, and the baby's heartbeat was mesmerizing. The rapid, *whoosh, whoosh, whoosh* had lulled me into deep thought as the room grew more dim and dreary. Link was a few feet away, lying on the couch. I knew he was there, but I still felt alone.

Slowly time inched forward, and my torment was periodically interrupted by the impatient, unsympathetic nurse who came in to check my progress. I was exhausted, but sleep had eluded me, and my large-handed nurse, who was in no way caring or gentle, was only contributing to my agony and making my night feel longer. She would come in, check my cervix with her "man hands," and leave. As the door would close behind her, the isolation returned.

The events of the previous weeks were replaying in my head, and it was crazy how things had declined so rapidly. I remembered sitting in the waiting room at the doctor's office as I reached for that magazine. Had God been preparing me for this hour? I could almost read the words on the page. With the image of the article etched in my mind, the story weighed heavily on my heart. God has a way of placing items in our path, which was evident because of all the magazines I could have picked up and all the articles I could have read. He aligned the events of that moment. He determined the chair I needed to sit in, the magazine I needed to pick up, and the article I needed to read. The heartbreak of the story was fresh in my mind, and the worry I had doused earlier returned.

Tears were streaming down my face. I wanted to scream. I wanted to rip the IV out of my arm and walk away from everything. "This is not in my plan, Lord." The words I said were silent, and my distress was unknown to Link. I was unable to feel the pains of labor, but the mental anguish I was feeling was overwhelming. The conversation with the specialist replayed in my head. He did not say "might have," he said, "will have." The baby "will have spina bifida or Down's, or. . ." The possibilities were numerous.

My fists were clenched, and the anger was building inside me. "Why would you do this to me, Lord?" This question was also silent, and my tears were unceasing. Wiping my eyes, I was determined to will the situation away. I thought of the judgment I had received from my grandma over my weight. If I was judged so harshly over my weight, how harsh would the condemnation be toward a child with a disability? *My family will not love a special needs child*, I thought, again overcome with fear. *What will I do? How will we ever make it through this?* I held onto the chance that the doctors could have made a mistake; after all, they were not God. My idol of perfection was on life support, but it was fighting to survive as I assured myself that this was a misdiagnosis.

Through a split in the curtain, I saw the first light of morning, and shortly after, things seemed to come alive in the hospital. I could see Link better in the new light but couldn't tell if he was sleeping or lying there in deep thought as I had been. I was unsure how to start a conversation about the situation and was ashamed of what I had been thinking.

Mid-morning, things were beginning to happen, and as the time to deliver the baby drew closer, my anxiety increased. When the doctor entered the room followed by the nurses, the chaos also increased. It was time to deliver, and amid the activity, I paused and looked over at Link. When I caught his eye, he looked back at me. "Tell me if there is something wrong with her when she comes out," I said. I was tearing up and trying to control the emotion in my voice. "Don't wait," I reiterated as my voice cracked. "You tell me as soon as she comes out." My plea was hanging heavy in the air, and I was unsure of what was about to transpire. I had no idea how my life would change, no clue how the cry of that baby girl, the cry that set the hospital staff in motion, would launch us on a journey for which we were both ill-prepared.

Doctors are not God. Like every other human on the planet, they can make mistakes. In a few short days, we would step out of this hospital thinking we had all the answers, but life rarely goes as planned. This chapter in life was closing, but the story of this tiny girl had just begun.

Afterthought

I look back at this time in my life, and I can see that this was the starting point of a journey God had set in motion. It was a path He would use to crush idols in my life and teach me to turn to Him. At this time, I still believed I had to be perfect to be worthy of love—a belief which drove my emotions on this long night. Not only did most of my family accept this girl, but they love her dearly. Satan used my fear against me that night, but God, once again, showed His sovereignty. In the years to come and even now, God uses this child to change everything in our lives for good. I can look back and know that if we had altered the Lord's plan in any way, we would not have the blessings of today.

Although abortion never crossed our minds in this situation, there are countless people in the world today living with that decision. While many do regret it, there is nothing they can do now except grieve the loss. Abortion is a decision that someone cannot unmake, and once made, it is a mistake Satan will use to make them feel unworthy of forgiveness.

The general opinion of Christians, whether unfounded or not, is one of condemnation.[31] While that is nearly impossible to change in the secular world, it should not be challenging to change among Christians. Women are sitting in church, those who are contemplating abortion and those who agonize over having had an abortion.[32] They are already convicted and don't need more judgment heaped on them. They need compassion, encouragement, and forgiveness.

God doesn't see sin on an up-and-down tier, from really bad to not so bad. God sees sin on an equal plane, and no sin is worse than the other. Lying is in the same sentence as murder in the Bible. Sin is sin. All sin must be washed by the blood of Jesus.

So, where are churches lacking when it comes to abortion care? There needs to be more compassion and outreach, and pastors need to remind their congregations that in God's eyes, gossip and judgment are comparable to abortion and other sins. There should be an ability for those living in the aftermath of abortion to speak out without being condemned. No one can change the past, but the future can be significantly impacted, especially if we can save lives.

If you face an unplanned pregnancy and contemplate abortion, please don't let fear influence your decision. The baby you carry is a child, not a blob of tissue, and there are other options. Christ will provide the way because He will strengthen you for every journey (Philippians 4:13).

If you had an abortion and struggle with feelings of loss and guilt, please know that God forgives—you need only ask.[33] We have an enemy who works to convince people that abortion is the only solution, and then he delights in the guilt and condemnation. Seek help from a pastor or Christian outreach, because you are not alone.

Faith Lesson: God will set us on journeys to remove idols in our lives. We must learn to trust in Him and not false idols.

Ranch Talk

When we were helping Ron work cattle, well before this pregnancy, my horse slipped and fell. She fell on her side, and my right leg was smashed by the saddle when she hit the ground. I remember jumping up and looking around to see if anyone had seen what happened. I was so worried about bruising my pride that I would have done anything to hide the incident. I could hardly get back on my mare because my ankle was throbbing. We had another hour or so of gathering, and the pain subsided to a dull ache as I rode. When we got to the corrals, I was not sure how I would handle the situation. We were branding that day, which meant hours of hustle and hard work. I was proud that I could hold my own in the branding pen, especially since I typically helped flank calves. The fear of the anticipated teasing and judgment I had created in my mind began building.

I rode into the pen and took my left foot out of the stirrup. I had been riding with my right foot out of the stirrup since the incident. Leaning forward, I grabbed the saddle horn and swung my left leg over the rump of my mare. I slowly lowered myself to the ground and bore my weight on my left leg. I was hoping I would be able to walk around, and it would stop aching, and that way, I could help brand. As I stepped forward, I knew right away that helping work the pen was not going to be possible because I could not put any weight on that leg.

I was embarrassed when Ron insisted that I sit and elevate my ankle, and when we got back to the house, he made me go to the hospital for an x-ray. I had sprained my ankle that day but had worried about my pride more. If I could have, I would have worked through the pain regardless of the possibility of exacerbating my injury.

In this accident, my pride was my idol. I was worried more about being embarrassed or what people thought of me than about the injury. My fear of judgment was more significant than my fear of the consequences.

Worshiping or relying on someone or something above God breaks the first commandment in Exodus 20:3 (NKJV) where the Lord says, "You shall have no other gods before Me." We are commanded not to have anything or make anything for ourselves to bow down to and worship. Our idols will stand in our way of God's purpose for our lives.

When you set something up in your life that is more important to you than God, it makes the Enemy happy. Satan will lull us to sleep with earthly pleasures or confidence in something other than the Lord because his ultimate goal is to keep us from the kingdom of heaven. If he is too late to keep you from salvation, then he will do everything in his power to prevent you from fulfilling the purpose God has for you.

Recognizing these idols is only part of the solution, however, because once you have determined what they are, you must also remove them. We love our idols because they make us happy and feel fulfilled, so how can we enjoy life without them, right?

One of the most profound things about the year 2020 is that we lost sports, restaurants, shopping, movies, and bars, and we still managed to survive. We need to remember that there is only one place to find comfort, and there is only One who can rescue us, and that is God.

Prayer

Heavenly Father, I come before You, understanding that there are items and distractions in this world that have my attention and earthly desire. I am aware of many of these, Lord, but realize there are things in my life I do not recognize as idols. Please reveal the things I am putting before You, Lord, and help me put these in their proper place. I know You do not want us to have a life devoid of happiness, but I also acknowledge that genuine joy can come only from You,

Father. I want to build my treasures in heaven, where I know they will not be stolen or destroyed. I pray this in Jesus' name, amen.

Study

Matthew 6:19–20 tells us that we need to build for ourselves treasures in heaven rather than on earth. Any material objects we have here on earth are eventually tattered and worn. Remember that purse you just had to have? The one you loved and was so expensive you had to save up to buy? Was that the same bag you gave to charity last week?

We all have things like this in our lives, and I am incredibly guilty of this problem. One of my issues has always been money or rather the lack thereof. God worked on me over my love of the almighty dollar and my pride for years until He finally had to break me down to nothing. Things did not begin to change in those areas of my life until I finally surrendered all of it to Him. A good indication that you have set something above God is when that thing becomes the center of your world. When you have something you think about continually and revolve your life around, then chances are it is an idol. Can the thing you are giving your attention and love to save you in times of tribulation? If it is not God, then the answer is no.

Look up and write out Isaiah 45:20. _____

_____

_____

_____

_____

_____

What will save you in your times of trouble? There is only One who can save you and keep you from harm, and I guarantee that it is not an earthly product. As told in the verse you just wrote out, we are ignorant to think our idols can save us.

Misplaced Faith

When we put our trust in money, we never have enough money. If it is a person, then they are often not there when we truly need them. Like every other human being, I struggle with idols, and I am by no means saying that we should not enjoy life. However, if something consumes us, we need to put it in the proper place, which is behind God.

List out things that consume your thoughts and time and take the place of God in your life. Examples could be money, sports, food, online shopping, games on your phone, news, Facebook, and so forth.

1. _____   6. _____
2. _____   7. _____
3. _____   8. _____
4. _____   9. _____
5. _____   10. _____

I once fasted from online shopping for thirty days. It was difficult, but it put my addiction into proper perspective.

From your list above, choose two things for a total of eight different "idols" and fill in the lines below. Fast from doing these things or obsessing about them for the designated amount of time.

Every week for 48 hours, I will not:
1._____   2. _____
For 7 days, I will not:
1._____   2. _____
For 14 days, I will not:
1._____   2. _____
For 30 days, I will not:
1._____   2. _____

Fasting from your idols is not easy, and you will be tested, but it is worth it. You will likely discover a whole new world, and if you commit that time to God, you will have a new understanding of the Lord and a better relationship with Him.

Forgiveness Takes Faith

*Be kind to one another, tenderhearted, forgiving one
another, as God in Christ forgave you.*
Ephesians 4:32 ESV

"I am sitting right here," I responded, "and I heard what you said."
My voice cracked, and all I could think to do was pick up my
"ugly" baby, gather Taylor, and leave.

When Forgiveness Is Hard

There are things in our lives we have no control over. These moments will come when we least expect them, and they can damage
us at our core, leaving a mark on our soul. If we harden our hearts
and are unable to forgive others' trespasses, we are only turning our
backs on God. When Christ endured the excruciating pain at the
cross, He did it for those who were calling for His death. When we
believe in the forgiveness of the Lord, we must be willing to extend
forgiveness to others. It is not easy at times, and we may falter, but
we must forgive.

Kaylee Ann was born at 10:15 a.m., and she did not have any physical features attributed to specific disabilities like Down syndrome. They immediately ran a tube down her throat, but everything was fine, so they did not have to rush her into surgery.

At four hours old, she stopped breathing, and they resuscitated her. She weighed five pounds, thirteen ounces and was only seventeen inches long. She was too weak to suck, and I had to pour milk from a cup into her mouth to feed her. The hospital discharged us after several days of tests and monitoring. Kaylee's head was in the fifth percentile, and she was still too weak to suck, but they marked "normal" on all the paperwork and sent us on our way.

With a false sense of security in thinking everything was fine with our baby girl, we walked out of the hospital's front doors financially broke. Other than the few dollars Link had in his pocket, we had eleven dollars in the bank, and we were two hours from home. There was no financial security, but God had given us a free roof over our heads and hope for the future.

Kaylee seemed so tiny, and she looked like a little peanut in her car seat. We got her home and promptly began to get into a new rhythm of life. Taylor loved her new little sister and was willing to help where she could. Kaylee cried a lot and screamed when we held her, so she spent most of her time in the rocking car seat. Link would take the early night shift, and I would get up around 1:00 a.m. for a shift change. We were still pouring milk out of a cup and into her mouth when she went for her first visit with Dr. Lindel.

The doctor did not seem overly concerned about her, and he assured us that the hospital had performed all testing, and everything looked good. Clueless, we went on with life, and I searched for a bottle with a nipple that Kaylee could suck on. It was an exhaustive search, and because of our limited funds, I stretched the hunt out over a long period.

Link was welding for the farmers again and had decided he wanted-ed to get a semi and start a trucking company. He had made friends with a man when working on the greenhouses, and they formed a plan. He started researching possible haul contracts, determining what it would take for success. He had always dreamed of owning a truck, and he wore a pencil out trying to convince me that it was a no-fail plan. I trusted him, even though this was no time to start a business. Regardless of the struggles we had faced in our past, he had always provided. Therefore, I reluctantly went along with his plan.

I had my hands full with Kaylee, and at one month old, the doctor diagnosed her with "failure-to-thrive." Bills were starting to add up quickly with diapers, endless bottle nipples, and now she needed specialized formula. We were still paying for our health insurance, and I made sure it was the first bill paid. But we were barely keeping our heads above water, and then the hospital bills started rolling in. We were sinking but were unable to gauge the depth of the water. It was not a good time to even think about starting a business, but being risk takers, we were not logical in that sense.

We slowly adapted to our new life with this baby girl and learned how to keep her content. She still screamed when we held her, and we would have to wrap her tight in a swaddling blanket before putting her in the crib or she would not sleep. But every day was a little easier. Link started calling her "peanut" because she was so tiny.

Every hospital and doctor bill that came in was another weight piled on our shoulders, but this was just the beginning. We had chosen a high-deductible plan because that was all we could afford, and that decision was haunting us now. It was all we could do to stay sane.

Link had moved forward with the trucking company, and with the help of family, he had purchased a semi and was hauling rock from a marble pit. He left the house early, drove all day, but was able to be home every night. With the added expenses of fuel and upkeep to the truck, however, we began to feel the financial burden tightening even more. We had leveraged every possession we owned to start this business and had family involved.

At three and a half months old, Dr. Lindel was worried about Kaylee's hips, so he sent her for an x-ray. Her hips had issues, nothing that required surgery, thankfully, but it added another bill to our ever-increasing pile.

Our living arrangement stayed the same, but we were still grieving Grandpa Ron's passing. Ron and May were such significant parts of our lives, and his absence left a large void. Peter had taken over all the ranch work for his father, Ron, and we helped him as much as we could. May and I became closer, and we began to spend more time together. When I went to town, I typically asked her to go with me. I considered her to be my best friend. But we were also under a new landlord now, and it felt as if they were making up jobs for us to perform. They seemed to have dreams of an inheritance from the landowner and were trying to prove their worth to him. They worked to increase not only our caretaker responsibilities but also our financial responsibilities.

It wasn't long before the people who owned the marble pit sold their business, and Link lost his contract. He then started working with a broker and was hauling loads between Phoenix and Las Vegas, Nevada. He was gone for weeks at a time, and I was alone as I worked through every new issue.

As Kaylee got older, her little personality developed. Her screaming subsided, and she was happier but still preferred to be alone in her crib. At around five months old, however, Kaylee started to have constipation issues. Right after she ate, she would try to have a bowel movement, and since her stomach was full, she would vomit up everything she had eaten. She would then choke as she took a deep breath. It was horrible, and all I could do was try to comfort her as I wiped away the vomit. It happened mid-morning every day and quickly became a routine I dreaded.

When the summer was over, the broker sent Link to northern Arizona. He was hauling cinder to the state yards for the impending icy road maintenance. The stress I was under dealing with Kaylee's issues on my own made me a ticking time bomb. The slightest deviation in plans or bump in the road would cause me to explode. Taylor lived in a war zone, and she did everything she could to help and try to keep the peace. It was too much to ask of a seven-year-old child, but I didn't see her pain. I was too wrapped up in my problems. I had high hopes that there would be a quick fix for Kaylee's constipation at her next doctor's appointment.

At Kaylee's next visit, I explained the issue to Dr. Lindel. I made sure he understood our new daily routine, or nightmare, rather. The pain she experienced, the straining, screaming and choking. I tried hard to emphasize the difficulty we both had with this as a part of our everyday lives, but he did not seem to hear my plea.

"Well, as long as she doesn't aspirate it," he said calmly, "I don't think there will be a problem." He seemed unconcerned and basically disinterested in our situation.

"How will I know if she aspirates it?" I asked, clueless what aspirate even meant.

He continued to speak in a slow, monotonous tone. "If she gets pneumonia, we will know," he said. "You can try giving her apple juice," he added before he turned and walked out.

I stood there thinking, *That's it, that's all you've got? I am living in hell on earth, and you give me that? You give me apple juice!*

I left his office, and on the way home, I stopped and bought some apple juice. I was still annoyed, but I clung to the hope that the apple juice would fix Kaylee's problem so life could be less complicated.

A month later, we were back in the doctor's office. The drama with the bowel movement was still our daily ritual, and I could almost set my clock by the episode. I started to become accustomed to just wiping the vomit from her face and crying while she screamed through the pain. I also continued to spiral down into a pit of bitterness and despair, growing angrier every day. However, I again walked into the doctor's examining room with high hopes that he would have an answer. I was sure that once he knew the juice did not work, he would give me a real solution. I remained convinced that there had to be some medication to fix our situation.

"Well, you can try prune juice," he said without even looking up from Kaylee's chart. "I am not as worried about that as I am at the size of her head."

I stared at him blankly as he continued, "I am going to be referring you to a neurologist in Tucson," he said, "because her head has not been growing as it should, and I am afraid her sutures may have closed prematurely." Again I stared at the door after he walked out. The issue with her head did not even register because I desperately needed my current problem solved. But no, I got "prune juice!"

I had walked in with high hopes and again received nothing. I struggled to determine why the doctor could not understand how dire our situation was and why he seemed unwilling to help. The unmet expectations left me feeling frustrated and alone. I felt like I was the only warrior in the battle, and I was losing the war.

So I stopped at the store on the way home to buy some prune juice. *What else?* I thought, as I pushed Kaylee in the cart around the store, *What else could possibly happen to make this worse?* I was oblivious to my surroundings and was deep in thought as I shopped. A woman walked up, smiling at Kaylee, and started talking to her. I smiled and looked at Kaylee, but she did not respond with any emotion, and as she looked at the lady, her expression did not change. Kaylee's response was typical because she was a rather serious baby and not prone to laughter or smiles.

The woman looked at me and said, "So what are we doing for her?"

I stared at her blankly, "Uh, what do you mean?" I asked the question with sincere ignorance and annoyance and thinking, *What's up with the "we" lady? Where have you been?*

"Well, she obviously has some developmental issues," she said. "Are you receiving any services for her?"

Because I was still living in denial, I was highly offended. "Well, the doctor hasn't said there is anything wrong." My statement was cold, and I didn't hide my annoyance in either my expression or demeanor, so she walked off. Angry and frustrated, I finished my shopping and left on the verge of tears. I picked up our forgotten child, Taylor, at school and headed home.

I continued to chip away at the bills every chance I had, and even if I only sent a small amount, I always sent something. I also continued to pay the insurance bill first because I could not imagine losing that. The stress was overwhelming, and Link was absent as he attempted to keep his dream alive. I noticed that his personality was changing, and for the first time in our marriage, he was losing his confidence. Taylor lived in a battle zone, because regardless of whether Link was home or gone, there was no peace. Every aspect of our lives had turmoil and uncertainty attached.

When I dropped Taylor off at school one morning, I noticed she hung her head as soon as she stepped through the gate. My heart sank, and I attempted to help her that afternoon, but all I could come up with was telling her not to hang her head for anyone. I didn't know what else to do. I couldn't help myself or Kaylee or Taylor, and instead of looking up to the only One who could help, I stubbornly moved forward in distress.

There are moments in our lives when we feel isolated and alone. Moments when we just want to sit in the corner of a room curled up in a ball, eyes closed, and heart hardened. Life can drive us into a state of submission. Do we turn and get back in the fight? Or raise the white flag and surrender? The war can be bloody and leave us wounded and scarred, but sitting in the corner will only delay the battle. When we seek an escape from our enemy, it doesn't mean we avoid the war, we have just delayed the fight.

Four months after Dr. Lindel's referral, we walked into the neurologist's waiting room. Even though we couldn't afford for Link to take a day off, I insisted he go with me because I was at my breaking point. I could no longer do this alone. It was a consultation, and we walked into his office and sat down in front of his desk.

The neurologist gave us a quick lesson on what happens when the sutures in a baby's head typically begin to fuse and the issues that come with premature fusion. Then he proceeded to book a CT scan, which would be four days after Kaylee's first birthday.

He looked up at both of us and at Kaylee, who I was holding on my lap. With a smug look on his face, he said, "You know we may just be dealing with an FLK."

Link and I looked at each other, then Link asked, "What is an FLK?"

"Funny looking kid," he said, as a smile spread across his face.

I closed my eyes and took a breath. I had expected this judgment the night I was waiting to deliver, and I had received a double dose in the recent months. I could tell the comment had affected Link also, but he kept his mouth shut, as did I. When we left the office and got into our pickup, I could tell Link was fuming, and a part of me was glad he had experienced a taste of what I had been going through.

"FLK," he said as we were getting in the truck. "Did you see the picture of his fat 'FLK' sitting on his desk?" We were both angry, and it was nice to be on the same side for a change. When we returned home, however, we returned to our battlefields, and the war raged on.

It was time for the CT scan. My mom went with me and helped me get her to the hospital. She sat in the back and kept Kaylee awake on the two-hour drive. It was hard watching my tiny girl go through the test, but we were happy to hear that the sutures had not closed, so surgery was off the table. However, the results we received only reinforced my belief there was absolutely nothing wrong with Kaylee.

Link and I were barely hanging on financially. At this point, we were underwater, but it was just something we did not acknowledge. The trucking continued to worsen, and I never really saw him because he was always on the road. His optimistic personality was vanishing, and I was worried about him, but my increasing bitterness kept me from letting him know my concern. He had always been the one who fixed things, and he seemed to have given up. Everything was beginning to fall around us, and I just wanted him to fix the problem. It was all going in the wrong direction. Everything was going wrong.

There are differing views on the origination of Murphy's Law. The Murphy's Law website has an excerpt from an article dated March 3, 1978, from *The Desert Wings*. Captain Edward A. Murphy was an engineer working on the Air Force Project MX981, which dealt with sudden deceleration and its effects on the human body.[34] It was an experiment that took place at Edward's Airforce Base in 1949. The Captain was supposedly referring to one of the technicians when he said, "If there is any way to do it wrong, he'll find it." There are varying views on this statement and who said it, but the pessimistic phrase that I grew up with was, "Whatever can go wrong will go wrong."

When the Lord is working, a lot can seem to go wrong, but again it is about perspective. I tend to panic at terrible news and often overreact under pressure. I wish I could say that I have become a rock over the years, but I cannot. I have grown and am better at handling these situations but not perfect. At this time, I was much like Chicken Little, and when the sky was falling, I was in full-blown panic mode. The trouble with running a trucking business on a shoestring budget is that you have to count on things breaking down. Link had failed to factor that probability into his calculations.

When anything goes wrong on a semi, it is expensive to fix. Link had started hauling for local farmers. He was home more, but the semi started having one problem after another. The first repair was when he blew a steer tire out on the interstate. It just went downhill from there, and when an O-ring blew, and he had to rebuild part of the engine. It was devastating. My dad helped him work on the engine, but the downtime was more than our fragile financial existence could bear. Coming back from this calamity would prove to be impossible.

When Link got the semi back on the road, we limped along for a while longer, but I knew I needed to find a job. I had only held a few jobs in my life at this point, but I started my search for something that would bring in extra money. My anger and disappointment were growing as someone I had placed so much faith in was failing.

In Luke 15:11–24, Jesus tells the story of the prodigal son. I can imagine what the father felt as he watched the child that he had placed so much hope in just walk away. I can see him standing there, eyes fixed on the horizon, hoping that his son would turn back. His trust dashed when the son kept walking, and every day that passed, his disappointment increased.

It can be hard to forgive. It can be incredibly challenging when the offender is someone we love and trust. When the son squanders his inheritance and returns to his father, he does not expect a warm welcome. However, the father is quick to forgive, and he is elated to see his son. The older brother is not happy at his return and hardens his heart in anger and jealousy.

From an outside perspective, it is easy to understand the feelings on both sides of the situation. When we are honest, we can agree that it would be a little hard to swallow. The older son is working, and he comes home to the sounds of a party. The father didn't even invite him to the party, and he just let him continue to work. However, from the father's perspective, he is just delighted to have his lost son home. It can be challenging at times, but it is important to forgive quickly. Forgiveness is for us more than for the person we are forgiving.[35] The faithful brother in the story lived in turmoil because he couldn't let go of the bitterness. When you continue to pick a scab off a wound, it never heals.

My wounds were insignificant at this point, and I had no idea that this was just the beginning. Since my recent existence had revolved so much around my youngest daughter, I jumped at the opportunity to spend time around extended family, and we all loaded up one weekend to escape reality and relax. However, I did not realize how fragile my emotional stability was, and I stepped onto the battlefield unprepared for the fight.

There are typically individual members in everyone's family, whether good or bad, who stand out above the rest. I had one great aunt who had lived quite the life, and she, in and of herself, was larger than life. When I was young, we would sit in front of the mirror together and stare at ourselves. My Aunt Hazel was a somewhat eccentric person, and she loved to tell stories from her past. She had never married, and during WWII, she was one of the women who welded in the shipyards. She was someone very special to me, but someone who never seemed to mind what came out of her mouth.

Many people had shown up to this family event, and a group of us were sitting around talking. The tiny house was full, and several kids played in the middle of the living room as the adults sat around and talked. Kaylee sat on the floor, watching the children play around her. She was not walking yet but was interested in the activity. I was sitting close to Aunt Hazel, listening to several different conversations and enjoying the day. Out of nowhere, I heard her say, "It's just such an ugly little thing." The words hit me as if she had just punched me in the face. I looked over at the woman who had such a strong presence in my young life, and when she looked at me, I could see the surprise on her face as she realized I had heard what she said.

The room grew quiet, and the attention was on us. My response was automatic as I replied to the comment, "I heard what you said."

She looked at me in shock, and I knew she immediately regretted what she had said by the look on her face. But it was too late, and the tears rolled down my face as I sat with everyone's eyes fixed on me.

It was my worst fear come true. I had known the night I laid in that hospital bed that this day would come.

"I am sitting right here," I reiterated, "and I heard what you said." My voice cracked, and I picked up my "ugly" baby, gathered Taylor, and left. My sister Dawn followed me out the door, trying to talk me off the cliff, but I couldn't go back into that house. I was inconsolable at this point, and poor Link was clueless. He had not been in the room, and I was so heartbroken I couldn't tell him what had happened, but he knew we needed to leave. I came expecting compassion and support, and I was leaving feeling broken and alone.

The pain quickly turned to anger, and my heart hardened. Shortly after that, Aunt Hazel ended up in the hospital, and she was dying. My sister Dawn called me and begged me to go see her. Aunt Hazel was sure she was dying because she had said those things about Kaylee.

I refused to go. I felt like Aunt Hazel had beaten me up enough, and my pride and anger kept me from driving up to see her. I was so angry and bitter over her insensitive words that I found myself stuck in a bog of unforgiveness.

Because I allowed myself to wallow in my self-pity and not move forward in compassion, I let the Enemy place a stain on my soul. The lifeline was there and all I needed to do was reach out and grab it, but I refused to look up. She passed away shortly after my sister's phone call, and I never got to see her again. I missed an opportunity to ask her if she knew Jesus as her Savior. I never got to tell her goodbye.

I went to her funeral with a bitter heart. No one talked about the incident, and I tucked it away and allowed it to fester. No one seemed to know it was there, and since it had mixed with resentment over all my circumstances, I couldn't even recognize it. When it bubbled to the surface, it did not have its own identity. I was emotionally unstable.

Afterthought

As a mature adult looking back, I know that attempting to start the trucking business in our position was very impractical. However, we have always been risk takers, so it seemed natural to us. Later we found out that life plans only work when aligned with God's. When you seek God's will and place your trust and efforts in His plan, things will fall into place. It doesn't mean you will be an overnight success or never have problems again, but perspective makes a difference. The glory is the Lord's, and we must realize that success isn't by our hand.

Eventually, the turmoil of those early days with Kaylee subsided, and things were a bit easier, but I was unrealistic in thinking the issues would go away. With a child, whether typical or not, your worries never wholly vanish. With a special needs child, the concerns become altered because like the child, they are not typical. It is the glasses you choose to look through that determine what you see. When I choose to see only the problems in front of me, I stop living. When I look through the glasses of doubt, I see only hardship and struggle. Those lenses focus on the chaos of life and amplify the stack of unpaid bills and unmet expectations. The other pair of glasses, however, the ones with lenses of faith, focus on hope and promise. Those lenses show the work of the Lord and illuminate His presence and glory. Those are the glasses that Elisha prayed the Lord would allow Gehazi to put on in 2 Kings 6:17. Through those lenses, he could see that the fight was God's, and His army of angels were on the front line.

It does not matter what circumstance you face in life because all that truly counts is your perspective and determination. With its struggles, life is a war, and we can only fight it one battle at a time. Sometimes we win and sometimes we lose, but we concede the victory if we step off the battlefield.

I had unknowingly surrendered to unforgiveness when I buried this pain, and it all surfaced as I was writing my story. I talked through the Aunt Hazel incident with four people, and my pain emerged each time. When I wrote this down, I sobbed uncontrollably. I had forgiven my aunt, but I had failed to forgive myself.

The person I am today wishes I could go back in time. I would have rushed up to see her and forgive her. I would have talked to her about salvation. When the people we love the most beat us up emotionally, they leave the deepest stains on our souls. Removing the stains only happens through forgiveness.[36] Jesus washed away the stain when I chose to forgive, but I cannot change the missed opportunity. I wish I would have told her that I loved her and forgave her.

If you are in this situation, I pray that my story will keep you from making my mistake. Regret is something that clings to us for a lifetime.

Faith Lesson: When we are quick to forgive, we will never miss opportunities that God places in front of us. We will be ready to share the good news of salvation and draw others to the most crucial forgiveness of all.

Ranch Talk

I showed an animal in 4-H every year at the fair; my older sisters were in 4-H, so I followed their lead. I started with sheep, and as I got older, I showed steers and horses. We would get our livestock projects when they were young and halterbreak them first (train them to lead). Dad would run them through the chute to get a halter with a long lead rope on them. It was our job to ease up to them and grab the lead rope. When this process first began, I would always get dragged around the pen. We were told not to let go of the lead rope. If you let your steer get free, it will continually try to run away. I would get dragged all over that pen, and it was not a small area, but I was determined not to let go of my animal.

I bought a Charolais cross steer one year, and for some teenage reason, I named him Boy George. That was the meanest steer I had ever owned, and none of them before or after came close to being as evil as he was. He was continually charging at me and running off and dragging me behind him.

As it got close to fair time, the 4-H club had a clipping day at a local ranch. I dreaded that day because I knew this steer would be impossible to manage. We loaded him in the front compartment of our stock trailer and hauled him to the clinic. As the day progressed, I was amazed at how good he was. The other steers were unmanageable, but Boy George was perfect. On the drive home, I felt more confident, and my worries about handling this steer at the fair had diminished tremendously.

When Dad backed in, he didn't back up to the alley, so I could not just open the gate and let him out. However, Boy George had been so cooperative I wasn't worried. I opened the rear gate and stepped in the trailer to open the front compartment and grab his lead rope. I opened the latch on the middle cut gate, and when I started to step in with him, he charged at me. As I moved out of his way, I let go of the gate so he could run out of the trailer. However, he had hit the gate as I let go, and it bounced off the side of the trailer and swung back and hit him in the head.

When he turned back toward me, he was mad. With the escape door latched, and the upper compartment gate closed, I had no place to go. All I could do was wedge myself in the corner of the compartment and wait for impact. It was quite the blow since he charged from the end of the trailer and then stood and continued to hit me with his head. He had me on the floor mat still working me over when my brother-in-law jumped in to help. He slapped him on the butt, and as Boy George turned to charge him, he missed stepping on my head by a fraction of an inch.

Well, my hopes for an uneventful fair were also unrealistic. Like the unmet expectations I experienced with Dr. Lindel. Boy George was also a disappointment. On one of the days we were there, a spectator came by and thought it would be funny to tease him with his hat. That steer threw me over the fence when I had to go in with him because he was mad. I was so happy to sell Boy George that year, thankful I did not have to deal with him any longer.

In general, life events do not end in an auction where we can sell off our problems. God calls us to forgive others. We are not allowed to slam the door and walk away. When we cannot let go of others' offenses, our wounds may scab over, but they will fester and grow, waiting for an opportunity to resurface. The Lord will not allow them to heal. There is a storm raging inside that will keep us from peace, and until we lay it down at the cross, we will not be whole. Forgiveness does not mean that you must go back to a situation and allow someone to abuse you physically, mentally, or emotionally. There are situations we need to remove ourselves from, but we must forgive. When living in unforgiveness, we are only hurting ourselves. It gives the Enemy an open door of attack, and he will seize the opportunity.

I have lived in unforgiveness, and I went for years without thinking about the event, and then out of nowhere, it bubbled to the surface. I found myself back in the war, but I was fighting myself. I was fighting a memory and picking a scab off a wound I refused to let heal. It was an offense I refused to forgive, and I was the only one still hurting.

We often refuse to pardon someone for their offenses because we do not believe they deserve forgiveness. That person goes about their life and may have no idea what they have done or even care they have hurt you. Some may enjoy the fact you are angry and wounded. Your anger and unforgiving heart does not affect them because those feelings only impact you. If I could encourage you to do one thing, it is this: Care enough about yourself to forgive.

Prayer

Heavenly Father, I come before You as someone who realizes I have unforgiveness in my heart. I know I cannot move forward and continue down this path. I know if I want to live in Your forgiveness, I must extend the same mercy to those who have wounded me. I cannot do this without Your help, Lord. Please soften my heart and help me to remember that we are all fighting a spiritual battle. I pray this in Jesus' name, amen.

Study

It is impossible to move forward and live a happy, healthy life without extending mercy to others. The Bible says that when we are unwilling to forgive others, the Father will not dismiss our sins. When we seek God's will and purpose in our lives, we have to be living for Him, which means we have to be willing to forgive.

Look up and write down Matthew 6:14–15. _____

_____

_____

_____

_____

_____

_____

_____

_____

Please write down the names of people you need to forgive and their offense.

NAME	OFFENSE

Set a prayer goal. Pray good things for each person every day for one week. It won't be easy at first, but as you do this, it will become easier. I promise.

If you are still having issues with someone at the end of the week, continue to pray until those feelings of unforgiveness are gone. If the thoughts and feelings return, then go back to praying. It is incredible when God removes this burden and sets you free.

Faith to Fight

*Fight the good fight for the true faith. Hold tightly to
the eternal life to which God has called you, which you
have declared so well before many witnesses.*
1 Timothy 6:12 NLT

"I began counting the seconds. My baby's body was stiff and unresponsive. I could hear a faint clicking noise, her teeth clenched, her throat tightened. I was unsure if she was breathing. I remembered the doctor's words, 'brain damage possible with a six-minute seizure.' I looked at the timer as it clicked over five minutes and felt paralyzed by fear, not knowing what to do."

The Stains from Battle

Many challenges come to us without warning. Some issues we face are due to our own unwise decisions, but there are other trials that some mistakenly believe to be entirely due to happenstance. The free will that God has given to each of us can be a blessing, but it can also be a curse. When we boldly step onto the battlefield with the nonbeliever, we cannot go unarmed. The unsaved have no rules of engagement, and there is no honor in their tactics. We will not survive without the armor of God to protect us.

The trucking company was dying, and we were drowning in debt, but I had found a promising job opening. I was unskilled in many areas, but there was one thing I did know how to do—ride horses. I found a job opening on a guest ranch, and I knew I would prefer that over flipping burgers. I am an introvert, but we were desperate and needed income, so I was bold as I fought for this position. Riding and caring for the horses didn't worry me, but being social and entertaining guests terrified me.

My first instruction from Mark, the barn boss, included not going above his authority to the guest ranch owner. All questions and problems would go to him, and he would decide what the owner needed to know. Because I had to fight for this job, I was determined to show my worth and quickly fell into a routine. Entertaining the guests was a skill that slowly became more natural for me, and I started to enjoy even that aspect of the job.

There were four different rides every day: a three-hour trail ride, a two-hour loping ride, a seven-hour day ride, and a one-hour afternoon ride. I took the day ride twice a week and was randomly assigned a ride for the rest of the week. There were several wranglers, the barn boss, and me, the only woman.

Mark was controlling, but he was also a flatterer, and the Enemy knew I craved affirmation. He was reasonably good looking and a shameless flirt. Flirting had always been my natural tendency, along with my need for praise. The Enemy knows our weaknesses, so my need-to-please personality quickly became an issue as I worked hard to prove my worth. Because I felt like a failure at home, I craved affirmation and attention, especially since Mark did not initially believe I could do the job. The trap was set, and I was about to fall into it.

Satan uses our weaknesses to try to destroy us, and that is why the Bible tells us to put on God's armor for our battle with the enemy. Ephesians 6:11 (esv) says, "Put on the whole armor of God, that you may be able to stand against the schemes of the devil." Eve, in the garden of Eden, was taken down by the flattering tongue of the serpent. The devil knew her weakness, and he lied to her so he could destroy her. The Enemy was using that scheme on me. Mark always had different jobs for me, so I didn't think anything of it when he wanted me to help him catch his and his wife's horses to take them to their house. When we put the horses up, he said he had to take a quick shower because he would be leaving work for a personal errand that afternoon. I felt awkward sitting on their couch in the silence of the living room, and at the moment, I had missed his intention. He seemed annoyed on the drive back to the barn at the guest ranch, but I pretended not to notice. I thought nothing of it when he told me not to tell his wife I was at the house, and life went on. Since nothing had happened between us, I didn't give it another thought.

As Christmas approached, a family came to the guest ranch with a special needs teenaged boy. This young man took a liking to me, and Mark thought it was fun to tease me about that. Not accustomed to being around a young man with developmental delays, I was nervous about taking him on a ride. This young man was loud, not shy in the least, and had raging hormones. Meeting them the night before the ride, I was unsure how I would handle his advances toward me, and I was nervous but willing to prove my worthiness as an employee.

When I woke up at midnight throwing up, I had a feeling of dread. I knew that Mark would be furious with me if I called in sick, but as the puking continued, I realized I had no choice. I set my alarm to call in at a decent hour and fretted for the rest of the day. I knew it would be unbearable when I returned.

I was right, and I kept my mouth shut through my punishment for not coming to work. I had developed a friendship with Mark and the other wranglers. After work, we would all sit and visit, and I shared many personal struggles with them. It felt good to have friendship, and it was almost therapeutic. However, that also gave Mark an advantage over me because he now knew my likes, dislikes, and fears. Mark made me take every ride assigned to the young man by his mother because I was afraid of that situation. It was initially uncomfortable, but I quickly learned how to handle his advances and enjoy his unique personality. God teaches us the most valuable lessons when things are difficult for us. If we are unwilling to step outside our comfort zone, then we are not growing. We need to have the faith to fight through the fear.

I had known Mark's wife, Ellen, most of my life. Her personality naturally draws people to her, and she was someone I enjoyed being around. She was funny, and I felt like we got along well together. She repeatedly told me how much Mark lied, which I thought was odd at the time. However, later I realized that many of the things he told me were little white lies, but I dismissed it. *What is the harm in a little lie?* I thought. I still enjoyed being at work, so it didn't matter that much.

Life on the home front was a different story. My need to prove I was a valuable employee to Mark did not sit well with Link, especially in our current situation. We were facing bankruptcy, and as Link's self-confidence plunged, my anger and disappointment increased. I began to dread my days off, because when Link and I were together, we fought. I could not discuss any issues at work without a vast war, so I kept my mouth shut.

We limped through the holidays and Kaylee's second birthday. She was not developing typically, but since Dr. Lindel told us that all babies develop differently, we decided not to worry. Kaylee was still not walking, and she preferred to be left alone in her crib. Her constipation was an ongoing issue but had not been a major daily event for a while.

About mid-spring, the trucking company died. We could no longer hold on, and found a bankruptcy lawyer. We filed on almost all of our past debt and most of the trucking debt. Things we didn't file on were our dually pickup and the loan that some of the family had co-signed. Turning in all of the collateral items was humiliating, and the process broke Link down even more. We were both mentally drained and could hardly be around each other without hurling accusations.

As I eventually realized that I could no longer live to keep Mark happy as my boss, I quickly lost any semblance of a sanctuary at work. Mark did not appreciate my enlightenment, and he made me take every day ride he could, but in the end, that served me well. I was away from the drama at the barn. However, it was disheartening to return from the seven-hour day ride and find that I had to feed the thirty-plus horses after unsaddling my day string. But I kept my grievance to myself because complaining only brought more torment. When it came time for my week-long vacation, I was happy to escape.

Link was fighting his own battles after losing the truck, and he was having a hard time letting go of the past. I did not feel like I could confide in him, so I kept my work issues to myself. We were fighting most of the time, and he did not trust me anymore. My "Mark-pleasing" had left a gaping wound in our marriage. It was a war on both battlefields. I felt utterly alone.

As summer approached, my niece got the position as a summer intern at the ranch. It was nice to have family there and took away some of the loneliness.

Mark backed off in an attempt not to reveal his petty bias against me. When Mark and Ellen were getting ready to take their vacation, I looked forward to the brief reprieve. With Mark gone, I would have more control over my schedule. However, during his absence, I had to take a couple of days off for a crisis at home, and I did not anticipate the chaos this would set in motion.

When I returned to work, my niece, another wrangler, and I went to the headquarters to move some horses back to the guest ranch. We each haltered several horses and were ponying them behind us as we rode back to the barn. Every wrangler carried a mobile phone in case of an emergency. When we were riding away from the corral, my niece's phone rang, and it was Mark. I could tell he was grilling her about something, and I had her hand me the phone. I was annoyed that he had not called me directly. My stress over this situation had been building for months, and I was close to losing my peace.

Volcanologists have discovered several factors that trigger a volcanic eruption, but two of the most important are increased pressure and magma.[37] I should have realized that I was on the brink of losing control with the increasing issues around me. Satan is a master at conflict, and he seizes every opportunity for division and destruction. He is observant and good at adding necessary elements for his desired results. Losing self-control never ends well.

When Mark began to berate me about taking some days off while he was on vacation, I could not stop the eruption. Unfortunately, right in front of my niece, I did not hold back. I released months of frustration, pain, and anger as his words detonated my ugly, expletive-filled explosion.

I knew there would be collateral damage from my loss of control; however, I did not anticipate the extent of the hatred Mark harbored toward me. After my initial fear wore off, I assumed everyone would calm down and move forward, but I could not have been more wrong. There are consequences for every action, but I was unaware of the train headed full steam ahead, and I was walking right down the middle of the track. The Bible says we will reap what we sow. Bad seeds were sown over the past year, and we would all reap of that harvest.

I despise the word "karma." When people steal from God's Word, and then society picks it up and uses it without knowledge of the origination, it annoys me. Galatians 6:7 (NKJV) says, "Do not be deceived, God is not mocked; for whatever a man sows, that he will also reap." If we plant bitterness and hatred, we will gather that to us. When someone lies in an attempt to defame another, they will reap from that lie. If we sow compassion, love, and understanding, then others will give us that in kind. Unfortunately, with every offense that we either sow or reap, it is harder to plant good things. It is much easier to become bitter and remain stuck in unforgiveness.

Too often, people expect to be forgiven for their trespasses but refuse to forgive others. That is an easy trap to fall into, especially for someone with no self-reflection and someone who does not take responsibility for their actions. We cannot walk around expecting to be pardoned from our offenses if we cannot extend a pardon to others.

In Matthew 18:21–35, Jesus tells the story of the unforgiving servant. Brought before the king because of his massive outstanding debt, the servant pleads for mercy. Out of compassion, the king forgives what this servant owes, which is ten thousand talents, equivalent to about six billion dollars.[38] However, when that same servant sees someone who owes him one hundred denarii, which is equal to about twelve thousand dollars, he is unwilling to forgive the debt and imprisons him. When fellow servants reported the events to the king, he rescinded the pardon of the unforgiving servant. The new punishment was torture until complete repayment of the debt. The one who loses the most in this parable is the one who is unwilling to forgive.

When Mark and Ellen returned from their vacation time, I falsely assumed things would return to normal. I had considered them both to be my friends. How big of an offense had it genuinely been to miss a couple of days of work? They knew the stress I faced at home, and I assumed my outburst was logical and forgivable. However, it did not take long to realize that I was inaccurate on those assumptions. When we quarrel with people who do not know God, we fight the devil himself. The unsaved do not engage in conflict under the same rules because they don't have the Holy Spirit to convict them.

I could understand why Mark was still angry since I had dared to challenge him, but I had no clue why Ellen would not speak to me.

After several attempts to mend the fences with them, I gave up and just did my job. At this time, I was unaware of Mark's offense and oblivious to the damaging lie he had uttered to Ellen. His successful defamation of my character caused collateral damage as it also imploded his world. I was unaware of the fact that Mark had accused me of seducing him into having an affair. I didn't learn about it until many years later.

As summer came to a close, things at work became more and more unsettled. My niece left for school, and when Ellen left Mark for another man, the tension continued to build. I felt bad for Mark. I could see he was trying to mend something shattered, and I felt compassion for him. I was still oblivious to the details of the breakup and Mark's accusation towards me.

If we are somewhere God does not want us to be, He will remove us from the situation. God put things into perspective the day I received a message at work about Kaylee. The babysitter had put her down for a nap and had difficulty waking her up, so she called 911. Kaylee was headed to the emergency room, so I left work to rush to the hospital. When I walked in, Link had already arrived, and we had no clue what was happening.

The doctor had evaluated her and was unsure what exactly the cause was, but he found nothing to be concerned about and sent us home. God had laid the groundwork to remove me from the job situation. When the Lord decides to propel us forward, there is no ignoring the signs. I had no other option at this point. I quit this job and turned my focus back on my family because I had a baby who desperately needed a mother.

I tried to put that job behind me, but the Enemy followed me home. My relationship with Link was still on rocky ground. It had taken a sharp decline with the turmoil surrounding Mark and Ellen, and I was still living on multiple battlefields. We reside in a small community, and the rumors of my supposed infidelity spread rapidly. I was the only person in the situation who knew nothing about Mark's deceptive lie. There was a festering sore in our marriage, and if the subject of my past job or Mark came up, Link exploded.

After each battle, we would apply a small Band-aid to the wound and move forward. However, the issue was still there, and since nothing had been resolved, it was something the Enemy would continue to use against us. This situation needed professional help, but we did not have the money for that, and the only thing holding us together was two precious girls.

As Taylor's birthday approached, Link and I called a truce and decided to take her to Tucson. We could not afford much, but we stayed in a low-budget motel and planned to visit local museums. We took one of Taylor's cousins with us, and the first day was fun. It felt like we were a cohesive family again.

That evening I noticed Kaylee had little energy, and assuming she was just tired from the day, I laid her down for bed. Soon after she fell asleep, I noticed something strange and called Link over to look at her. He immediately grabbed her up and carried her out the door toward the lobby. Panic-stricken, I grabbed my purse, gathered the girls, and headed to the hotel lobby. The ambulance had arrived, and they were assessing Kaylee. They determined she needed to go to the emergency room, and I got in the ambulance to ride with her. After several hours, they gave her antibiotics and discharged her.

When we followed up with Dr. Lindel, he was again of little help. I sat in the exam room, and he looked at me and said, "These are just febrile seizures, and as long as it doesn't go over six minutes, there will not be any brain damage." I again stared at him blankly.

"I can send her to a neurologist if you insist," he said, "but I don't think it is necessary."

"I insist," I said. My patience was gone.

Dr. Lindel sent my two-year-old baby to an adult neurologist, and the only good thing that came out of the appointment was an actual diagnosis. We also received a call from a family friend who convinced us to take Kaylee to a Tucson doctor. It was a three-hour drive from our house to Dr. Roberts' office, but we began the process.

As we waited for the day of our appointment with the new doctor, I noticed that Kaylee was falling more. The seizure activity was increasing, accompanied by her falling and hitting her head. Her fear of being alone and going to sleep in her crib also increased.

In early December, she started the day with an early morning fall and hit her head on the floor. She continued to stumble and fall when we were outside, and by mid-morning, I laid her on the couch for a nap. She was unwilling to be laid down in her crib.

When I looked over at her, after she had been asleep a few minutes, I could tell something was wrong and realized she was having a seizure. I began counting the seconds, which turned into minutes. My baby's body was stiff and unresponsive. I could hear a faint clicking noise, her teeth clenched, her throat tightened. I was unsure if she was breathing. I remembered the doctor's words, "brain damage possible with a six-minute seizure." As I worked to cool her body down, I took note of the time. When the timer clicked over five minutes, I felt paralyzed by fear, not knowing what to do. It was the most prolonged seizure I had seen her have. I ditched the watch and called Link. When I picked Kaylee up to go, I noticed that the left side of her face was drooping, and panic wanted to take over, but I suppressed it.

Link was waiting when we arrived at the hospital, and he carried her into the ER reception area. Dr. Lindel was on duty that day, but he refused to come in and see her. The nurses gave us a prescription for a seizure medication and, surprisingly, sent us on our way.

Link called the new doctor's office to see if we should fill the prescription. Dr. Roberts wanted her on the medication, and we were so thankful that Kaylee's first visit with him was just a couple of days away. When Kaylee started seizing again, Link picked her up and headed back to the emergency room.

Dr. Lindel graced us with his presence on the second visit. He said, "Well, you know Kaylee has been telling me she would do this all along, and I was just waiting to see if this would happen." Dr. Lindel knew Kaylee had significant medical issues, but he chose to ignore the problem. Frustrated, I walked over to Lindel's office to attempt to get her medical records. I was afraid it would take several weeks to receive them, but by a miracle of God, they printed them off while I waited and gave them to me. I was happy I would never see Dr. Lindel again.

When Dr. Roberts saw Kaylee, he was so concerned he sent her to the hospital for three days of testing. It was a relief someone was listening, and we had found a doctor who was as concerned as we were about Kaylee's condition.

A month or so after the seizures, a new doctor, and a hospital stay, we received a letter from our insurance company. You know the one, the insurance that was the top priority. The bill that took precedence over every other bill and got paid first? Well, they had decided to send our payment back and cancel our policy. They were happy to take our money until things began to get tough.

Afterthought

When we run from God's will for our lives, we enter into a war. We may not see the armies fighting, but there is a spiritual battle raging around us. I stepped onto the battlefield without God's armor, and because I was not prepared, it altered my character. I stepped into the war naïve and trusting and exited bloody and bruised, my trust fractured and my soul stained. Stepping into the next skirmish, I appeared clean, having washed off the blood from the last conflict, but the blemish remained. It didn't matter how much I treated that stain with my worldly strength because it kept coming back. The stains we have on our souls come by way of others' words and actions and by things entirely out of our control. We may cover them up and attempt to scrub them away, but they gradually resurface. When we don't forgive others, Satan uses our hardness of heart and bitterness to cause those stains to reemerge.

God always takes care of us, even when we stray, and He leaves the flock to gather us and place us back under His protection (Matthew 18:12). I was so thankful for Dr. Roberts because he genuinely cared about Kaylee's well-being, and we needed a trusted ally. Link and I joined together to fight for Kaylee, but there was a deep divide in our marriage. I had not had an affair with Mark, so I was unaware I needed to fight that battle. I kept scrubbing at a stain but couldn't see what it was, so how could I remove it? The stain was a false accusation of adultery. It is impossible to fight something you can't see. The devil was smiling, and he kept things stirred up. It finally dawned on me that I had received the blame for breaking up a marriage, but I still didn't know I wore the scarlet letter of adultery.

However, God can redeem us from everything, even things of which we are unaware. For a couple of years, I sold real estate, and one of my mothers-in-law was my broker. I have three mothers-in-law. We affectionately refer to them as "the one who had Link, the one who raised him, and the one his dad is married to now." My mother-in-law, the one who was my broker, is the one who is married to Link's dad now.

We were both sitting in our separate offices one day when a man named Jim walked in. I knew him but not well, so I was surprised when he sat down at my desk. Jim told me that he worked with Mark's ex-wife Ellen, and he had a question to ask me.

Reluctantly, I said, "Okay, ask."

"Ellen told me," he said, "the reason she is leaving her current husband, Kyle, is because he is having an affair with you." She was leaving her second husband, and, according to her, I was again the cause of the breakup.

I had been spending my days in that office, and this time I had a witness to account for my time and actions. The statement was laughable. "Did you hear that?" I said to my mother-in-law, "I am having an affair."

"I don't know when you are finding the time for that," she said, "since you are here with me all day and home at night."

We have no power to stop accusations and no ability to redeem ourselves. Our redemption is in the Lord. Exodus 14:14 tells us to be still and do nothing to defend ourselves because God will vindicate us.

I guess I am relatively "thick" because Mark's offense didn't dawn on me until years later. Link and I were sitting watching TV one night, and it just hit me.

I looked at Link and said, "Mark set me up."

Link said, "What do you mean?"

"The day he made me take the horses to his house," I said. "He set me up. He must have told Ellen something else happened."

I could see that it also registered on Link's face, and I knew I was right. Mark, in his anger, had lied and told Ellen that we had committed adultery that day. With accusations of adultery, I'm sure Ellen received sympathy and validation when leaving Mark for another man, and she was continuing to perpetuate the lie all these years later.

God used Jim the day he walked into the office to pardon me. I didn't see it at the time, but his boldness in asking me that question, along with my mother-in-law's witness, exonerated me in the eyes of the world. However, I was still guilty.

Matthew 5:28 says that anyone who looks at another person lustfully has sinned. If you are married, you have committed adultery in your heart, and if you are single, you are guilty of fornication.

So in God's eyes, I am guilty of adultery, as is most of the married population. I am not an innocent victim because I did find him attractive, and I did crave his attention and affirmation, and I did flirt with him. I let the devil lead me down a road that could have ultimately led to the physical act of adultery. When we walk that line, we are on a dangerous path of destruction. It was God's grace that guided me out of that situation, and nothing in my power can exonerate me from the sin of what was in my heart. We need the blood of Jesus because we have all sinned and fall short of the glory of God (Romans 3:23).

We must remember that the Enemy will use even a slight imperfection to bring us down. He knows our weaknesses, and mine involved validation and attention from others, especially men. Removing that stronghold in my life has taken years of praying and changing. The Enemy can have a powerful grip on us through our shortcomings, but destroying that hold can come only with God's help.

The unsaved are without any hope, and they have no promise of treasure beyond this life. That is why people who do not know the Lord operate only for themselves and have no regard for others. The rewards and treasures they obtain on this earth are all they get because they have no treasures in heaven. It is my hope and prayer that, if they have not already, both Mark and Ellen will find the redeeming love and forgiveness of the Lord. I pray this for all the unsaved in this world.

Satan is in the business of destroying lives because he is going down and wants to take others with him. Our only weapon against him is prayer since God is the only one powerful enough to fight him. We are the light of the world because we have the light of life, and there is no darkness where the light shines (John 8:12).

Faith Lesson: God is the ultimate Defender. He is the only one able to pardon us from our sins.

Ranch Talk

I was the youngest of five girls, and much to my dad's dismay, I had no brothers. One of my favorite relatives was my great Uncle Alvin, my grandma's brother. He had a twin brother, and they grew up to be two tough cowboys. Uncle Alvin was a walking history book. He had a ton of stories about working on cattle ranches and in the mines. In World War II, he was in the 45th Infantry Division, which landed on Sainte Maxime beach on August 5, 1944, liberating southern France. On April 29, 1945, his 45th Division freed inmates detained in Dachau's main camp, the first Nazi camp that did medical experiments on inmates. His division was the first to arrive, and they found over thirty corpse-filled railroad cars. Inside the camp were more bodies and thirty thousand survivors on the verge of death.[39]

Uncle Alvin would come to stay at the ranch often, especially during spring and fall works. He was thin, wiry, and full of life. Alvin had a great sense of humor and loved to tell stories. He was an awesome man, and I loved him dearly. Around age nine, I decided I wanted to be an actress, and I was always practicing crying on cue in preparation for my future screen test.

One day, Uncle Alvin decided to walk to the top of the hill behind our house and check the cement tank. I tagged along barefoot, which was normal for me because I never wore shoes except to town. We took a trail the cattle had used so often they had worn a groove in the dirt, and it was powdery and soft. It weaved back and forth up the side of the hill, which made the climb easier. When Uncle Alvin was ready to head back to the house, I came up with a devious scheme. I started crying and telling him that I could not walk down the hill because my feet hurt. Well, I must have been convincing because he carried me on his back down that hill, and when he sat me down on the ground, I started laughing. What a brat I was.

Uncle Alvin told me that story every time I visited him for the rest of his life. I can still hear him laughing about it. He was one of the greatest men I knew. I felt embarrassed when he told the story, but I am so thankful that I have those memories of him. He was my favorite uncle.

However, a lie is a lie. This is a fond memory, but it is still about a lie. Mark told the lie that Satan used to shatter lives. The Enemy succeeded to some degree, but thankfully not where Link and I are concerned. Satan took the weakness I had for flattery and attention and set a trap. He used Mark's anger, his pride, and his desire for control to put that lie in motion. The only difference between Link and myself and Mark and Ellen is God. Link and I are the only ones under the Lord's protection.

When we put on the armor of God, we have protection from the battle. It is the Lord's mighty power that gives us strength. Read Ephesians 6:10–18 to learn more about the armor of God.

Prayer

Thank You, Lord, for Your continued work in my life. Thank You for continuing to make me the person You want me to be. I know I will never be perfect, but I am thankful for my weaknesses. I know my flaws highlight Your glory, Lord. Please continue Your work in me, heavenly Father, and help me to forgive as You have forgiven me. Please remove the stains on my soul, Lord. I pray this in Jesus' name, amen.

Study

We continue to work on forgiveness in this chapter. Until we completely release those who have wounded us, we cannot move forward. Forgiveness does not mean we have to go back to abuse or a dysfunctional relationship. However, forgiveness will release us from the bondage we are in over what has happened. It removes the hold the Enemy has over us. God has a plan for each of us, so we need to strive toward fulfilling our purpose.

Look up and write down Ephesians 4:32. _____

_____

_____

_____

_____

Now let's go over what we have worked through in previous chapters. We wrote down "I-am" statements, core values, and releasing fear and worry. We prayed for help from the Lord and acknowledged His blessings and intercessions in our lives. We fasted from idols and are working on forgiveness.

Write a letter to each of your offenders. You don't have to send it to them, but you need to write it out and release it. You can place these in an envelope and open them up in a month or so. I promise you will be amazed at the difference in your attitude.

Healing through writing is a fairly common tactic. I didn't fully realize the power in writing things out until I started writing this book. If you have the time and drive to do it, I encourage you to write your story. Write with honesty, however, because that is the key to healing. We have to acknowledge our responsibility, so write as if the world will read it.

The Faith to Surrender

And the vessel that he made of clay was marred in the
hand of the potter; so he made it again into another
vessel, as it seemed good to the potter to make.
Jeremiah 18:4 NKJV

"I was at my wit's end. We had given everything we had to this endeavor, and it was failing. Once again, it didn't seem to matter how much thought, effort, and money we put toward the dream; it was getting ready to fall, and we were back in the same predicament as before. We were going to lose our house, possibly everything."

Refined by His Hand

In Jeremiah 18:4, God is described as a potter. The verse makes it clear that He molds, shapes, and controls everything. It was God who determined what would happen to His people. The Lord sent Jeremiah with a warning to the house of Israel, but the people rejected Jeremiah's words. Like working with clay, things can get messy when the Lord is shaping and reshaping the nations and us. We, as followers of Christ, can surrender to His will or fight against the process. Fighting will bring hardships, but we are a stubborn lot. It is human nature to resist change and things that challenge us. The funny thing is that when we refuse to listen, the challenge becomes more significant and much more difficult.

Marriage is a challenging process, but so is life in general. It is a road full of twists and turns and can feel perilous at times. When we open ourselves up to the danger of failure, it can feel risky. It seems logical sometimes to abandon the initial foundation we are building on and start over. However, when we stand at a crossroads in life, forced to determine a route, it is dangerous to be impulsive. The danger involved pertains to every situation we, as humans, can find ourselves facing, and the road we travel is imperative to the outcome. Like the Israelites who wandered in the wilderness for forty years, decisions and attitudes have an impact.

Often when people face difficult situations, they feel they are just unlucky. The thought that a "mojo" binds us and follows us around is depressing and has caused many people to abandon their hopes and dreams. When we discard the concept of "luck," our eyes are opened to the fact that we are each a work in progress. God is the perfect Potter, and He is working to refine His children.

Link and I were licking our wounds. With the bankruptcy and the broken trust between us, we could hardly be around each other without bickering. We had never had a problem expressing our opinions to each other, but with the disappointment and false accusations of adultery, of which I was still unaware, it was nonstop fighting. When Satan finds a crack, he works to make the divide deeper. But the Potter can fix anything as long as the clay is still malleable. As an amateur potter, I can attest to the fact that this can be a tedious process.

Anytime you work with clay, you can repair defects as long as the clay has moisture and can still be made soft and malleable. When it becomes bone dry, it is beyond refinement unless you break it completely down and start over. When it goes through the first firing, it becomes bisque, and at this point, it is hard and beyond reclaiming.

Link and I were not beyond repair, but we were resisting the hand of the Potter. We needed to look up and submit, but we remained focused on our pain.

Link had taken a job at the county, but it kept us poverty-stricken, especially since we did not abandon all of our debt in the bankruptcy process. Since my income was gone entirely, we started to drown again, so he began welding for the local farmers on weekends.

In the fall of 2002, all of us girls enrolled in school. Taylor went back to her school, Kaylee started preschool at three, and I returned to college. I knew a degree was something no one could take from me. I helped a lady from church get certified to keep Kaylee in the afternoon, and Taylor went to Grandma May's. My efforts paid off, and things ran smoothly in my education plan, but that was all that was smooth.

Our finances and marriage remained on life support, and the stress was almost too much to bear. To help our financial situation, Link found a construction job in Tucson. He was skilled in running equipment and was hired on as a lead blade operator. The money was good, but the job was two hours from the house, so the girls and I were alone again.

With nothing repaired in our marriage, and with him still believing I had cheated, his absence only increased our division. He had escaped the reality of our circumstances this time and was quickly finding new interests to fill the hurt in his heart that I was unaware existed. Satan was working many angles to keep us apart, and the cloth that held us together was ripped and unraveling quickly.

For well over a year, Link was an absent figure in our lives. He lived with his biological mother, "the one who had him," and he had somewhat forgotten his family. His life revolved around his new job and his increased access to everything in the horse world. He was roping, learning to cut, and living an alternative life.

But God didn't quit on us, and when I began to push Link for change, the Lord stepped into action. In the summer of 2004, a real estate agent who had made a business leasing to own properties had a house with ten acres available. We jumped at the chance of owning a home, and it was a bonus that it had the property for our horses. Link was in love with the barn, but the house left a lot to be desired. I was willing to overlook the fact that I was moving into an old, ugly single-wide trailer because I was desperate to repair my life and marriage. I also believed that moving closer to Tucson would be better for Kaylee. She needed several therapy services, and I hoped that the opportunities and choice of providers would increase.

We worked hard to bury our past mistakes, and the farther the guest ranch days were in our rearview mirror, the more cohesive life became. However, the solidarity was misleading, and the questions Link faced about my unfaithfulness still gnawed at him. There were people around him who would not let the matter rest, and it was a cancer eating at the foundation of our marriage. But on the surface, everything seemed to be falling into place.

I tolerated the single wide for almost two years, and the road we traveled for a time was smooth. I had a real estate license now, and we were doing better financially, so we decided to put a new home on our property. It wasn't going to be anything fancy, but it would be better than what we had.

We started looking for used mobile homes and finally found one we liked. Honestly, I just wanted something better than what we had. We started the loan process, and everything looked good, but the loan would not go through for some reason. It was frustrating, and the loan officer had no idea why things were not falling into place. Every time I spoke with the loan officer on the phone, he had no answers. So we finally gave up.

God works in mysterious ways, and He always works for the good of those who love Him. Sometimes we need to lay aside what we want in order to receive His blessing. But we were still attempting to do things our way and not learning the lesson from God. Thankfully the Lord is patient.

After we abandoned our plan, we got an offer we couldn't refuse. A developer desired our property for access to a large piece of land behind us. They just wanted the land, and we could remove everything, including Link's beloved barn. We entered into the contract with a promise of a quick closing, but beware the promises of man. The property deal was just one of many troubles brewing.

When the fall of 2006 drew near, and it was time for the girls to go back to school, I was unsure about Kaylee's new teacher. I had issues from the beginning, and she was condescending and rude. Even though Kaylee was now seven years old, she had significantly delayed speech. She was only saying one or two words, and she could not tell me there was an issue. She had been riding the bus and loved the aid and the bus driver, so it wasn't until I went to pick her up early from school that I realized there was a problem with more than just my relationship with the new teacher.

When I stepped into the classroom, Kaylee came running toward me, holding her arm. My suspicions heightened when the teacher immediately began to justify the action. "She must have hit her arm when she came around the corner," she said. The problem was there was no corner: nothing to come around, and nothing to hit her arm on. I left the classroom with doubt and questions, and I knew I couldn't send her back without answers.

With guidance from a state advocate, I insisted on an IEP (individualized education plan) meeting. The day I showed up at the school, I had Kaylee with me. An independent state provider who had been working with Kaylee met us in the parking lot. Together we started walking toward the school grounds, and I was shocked when

Kaylee started screaming and attempting to run back to the car. I could not physically force her to go into the school, so the provider took her to the park.

The meeting was packed. The teacher and the aid were there, along with the school principal and psychologist. I was there with the advocate. The information that came out in the meeting was shocking. I was reasonably sure that the teacher had grabbed Kaylee by the arm, but I had no proof and no idea of what was truly happening. Since there was a written log coming home in Kaylee's backpack every day, I thought I was informed but realized I was rather clueless.

Kaylee's constipation issues did not just magically go away, and I had falsely assumed the special needs staff would know how to handle that properly. The aid in the classroom and the teacher were placing Kaylee on the toilet for thirty minutes at a time. If she had an accident, they, in their wisdom, were making her wash her underwear out, and then she was in time out for fifteen minutes. That didn't work because she loved to play in the water, and they felt she was enjoying the punishment too much. So yes, the staff at the school were letting my daughter play in feces-filled water. I was sending Kaylee to school for nonstop punishment where she was sitting on the toilet or in time out for most of the day. They felt she was maliciously having toileting accidents. I walked out of the school furious and feeling defeated. Kaylee never returned to that classroom, and we opted to enroll her in a local charter school.

The struggle with getting the property sold to the developers had been continuous also. So, I was not only dealing with the frustrations with the school but also our prospective buyers. I felt as if we were cursed and doomed to live a life of chaos and disorder. There had been several addendums to the contract, but we finally headed to the closing table. After we sat down, it didn't take long to realize we would not be signing papers that day. Another issue for the buyers had come up, and we started to suspect they were stalling. We drove home annoyed and empty-handed, but we agreed to extend the closing.

Disappointed and angry, I felt like everything in my life was spinning out of control. It is maddening to have something within your grasp, but you can only touch it with the tip of your finger.

Thinking things could not get worse, I received another call from the realtor. He informed me of an eleventh addendum to the contract and needed my signature on the form. I agreed to drive the fifteen minutes to meet him, and when I sat in my car, I was on the verge of tears. Nothing seemed to be working in our favor lately—Kaylee's school, the house we had attempted to purchase, and now selling this property. My tank was empty, and I was running on emotions, the greatest of which was despair fueled by disappointment.

I put my car in gear and burst into tears. "I give up, God," I said. "I don't know what else to do, and nothing is working for us." My statement was audible, and my voice cracked as tears streamed down my face. "What do you want from us? Why won't you help us?"

With my last question, a feeling came over me, and these responses entered my mind, *Have you asked for help? Have you worshiped Me? Have you glorified Me?*

I had not done any of those things. Through tears and at the height of my voice, I praised God. It was not pretty, and it was not perfect (because I cannot sing) but I did not let that stop me. I belted out the lyrics to the song, "God is good, all the time," for the entire drive. I didn't care who was watching because I was alone with the Lord singing His praises.

I looked a mess when I pulled up to sign the papers. The conversation was minimal, and when I drove off, I started singing the song again. "Your will be done, God," I said. "I trust You." I felt a great relief overcome me. I truly meant it, and I was willing to trust God's will.

The next time we sat at the closing table, we closed the deal. God had placed an attitude of "close or we walk" in me. They needed the property, and they didn't want us to walk away. We closed for more than the property was worth, and we would be able to take what we wanted with us.

When God brokers a deal, it is perfect. It wasn't long before I realized why the loan on the other house would not go through. If we had put that used double-wide on our old property, we would not have been in the position to sell.

As we settled into our new home, I forgot something. I forgot God again. I didn't turn away from the Lord, but I also did not turn to Him every day. I was back to being a crisis worshiper, a person who calls out to God in times of trouble but sticks Him on the shelf when the seas are calm. Instead of spending time with the Lord every morning, I found earthly pleasures. I found idols, like television and crafts, to receive my attention and affection.

Because we had sold the property for a good profit, things were going pretty well. Link had started selling real estate in his spare time, and he was working on some ranch deals, which could generate massive commissions—when and if they closed, that is. It didn't take long for us to spend our reserve of money and return to living paycheck to paycheck.

So what did Link and I do when things got tight financially? I decided to start a business with my sister, Dawn. We founded a company that provides children's services to special needs kids. Dawn's daughter-in-law had a business like this, and she was kind enough to help us get started. I had consulted Link, but I failed to consult the only One who mattered. I forgot to pray.

Link finally closed a ranch deal, and we used all of the fifteen-thousand-dollar commission for our portion of the starter money. We had again placed everything we had on an opportunity, and now we were officially back to barely-scraping-by status. If we failed, we would lose everything, but as usual, Link and I were not the ones to shy away from risk.

We struggled for years, and my sister and I worked with no pay.

Every dime we made went back into the business. After four years, we finally wrote ourselves a check, and that was a day of celebration. We each received a four-thousand-dollar check, and we were excited. That only worked out to $17.85 a week for 224 weeks of forty-plus hours of work, but we were excited, nonetheless. When we finally took consistent paychecks, things were not much better. My year-to-date pay one year in October was a little over one thousand dollars, so my income went up to twenty-seven dollars a week. We were struggling, and I was on call 24/7. If someone couldn't cover a shift, I had to cover it, and it was typically without pay. Because I still had God on the shelf and was attempting to make things work with my feeble abilities, the company was floundering. Without God, we were unable to succeed.

God molded the first human, Adam, from the dust or clay of the earth, and Job, Isaiah, and Jeremiah all referred to the connections humans have to clay. In Job 10:8–9 (CSB), Job says to God, "Your hands shaped me and formed me. Will you now turn and destroy me? Please remember that you formed me like clay. Will you now return me to dust?"

God is a divine Potter, and just as an earthly potter makes a vessel for a purpose, God has made each of us for His purpose. God reshapes us with His hands, and He prepares us for the calling He has placed on our lives. We each have a unique journey and a God-given appointment in our existence. God knows everything before we are even born, and He knows the day we will enter this earth and the day we will exit.

When we acknowledge we are here not for our selfish desires but rather God's perfect plan, we can see things differently. We begin to understand that the trials we face have a divine intention behind them. We may exit this earth, never knowing the lives we touched or how God used us to bring someone to salvation. Our one purpose in life could be leading just one other human to forgiveness in Christ.

That does not mean our suffering or loss is easy, but understanding there is a purpose will make it more bearable.

The loss of a loved one, for example, is devastating, but the impact that the death of one believer can make on society is tremendous. I have known people who have died young, but their love for the Lord sent shockwaves throughout the community. As Christians, we are not here for ourselves but to do God's work. Our days on this earth may be many or few, but they are not ours. That does not mean the Lord does not want us to enjoy life, but we must remember the job we have to do.

When we know the Lord, we understand our lives on this earth are temporary and fleeting, but heaven is eternal. Salvation is our only promise of an eternity with the ones we love. Suffering is not fun by any means, but the more we resist God's will, the more painful the process.

As we floundered, we started selling things off to make our house payment. We were falling further and further behind. The day the bank sent an assessor out so they could foreclose on our new home, I cried. Link was still working his construction job and real estate, but it wasn't enough with the business and the bills.

I was at my wit's end. We had given everything we had to this endeavor, and it was failing. Once again, it didn't seem to matter how much thought, effort, and money we put toward the dream, it was getting ready to fall, and we were back in the same predicament as before. We were going to lose our house, possibly everything.

I laid down in bed the night the assessor had visited our property, and when my head hit the pillow, I was silently crying. The seas were rough, and I again reached for God. But this time, I took Him off the shelf and have never put Him back.

Through my tears, I said, "You gave us this house, God, and if You want to take it, then take it, I guess." I finally gave it to God. "I trust You, God," I said. "I know that if you take this away, You have something better for us."

I felt a rush of relief when I realized the responsibility for success was not on our shoulders. Only God could make our endeavors successful, and He would only do that when we were actively seeking His will. I had finally surrendered to the hand of the Potter, and He was reshaping me into a new vessel.

Afterthought

When we submit to the Potter, our path is made clear. Proverbs 3:6 (NLT) says, "Seek his will in all you do, and he will show you which path to take." It takes thoughtful prayer and reflection to move toward the work God has for you.

I know not everyone has a call to be a missionary, but we are here to make at least a ripple in the pond. As believers, we are all part of the body of Christ, and we all have a purpose. Life on this earth is short compared to eternity, and we need to live for God. When I stand before God, I desire to hear, "Well done, my good and faithful servant" (Matthew 25:21 NLT).

The night I surrendered to God was the night when everything began to change. Right after I cried out, God started opening new doors for our children's services company. The tiny, struggling, one-town, one-building business that only served seven children, began to grow. We have moved into six cities and have eight sites helping hundreds of kids now, and all the glory goes to God.

Before I could crawl out of my pit of despair, though, I had to change my perception. I was looking to Link and money to rescue me and make me happy, and I was trying to do everything on my own. But what I really needed was God. To be clear, I understand people who are clinically depressed need medication, and if that is you, I urge you to seek professional help. I was not clinically depressed. I needed to change the lenses in my glasses, and as I was able to look back on past situations, I saw God's handiwork.

Our struggles did not magically disappear, but our responses to them changed drastically. When we attempted to open a door that God did not want to be opened, He would shut it and we didn't fall apart. Revelation 3:7–8 says that God knows our deeds and that He opens and closes doors. These verses make it clear that no one can open or close the doors but God. We now seek the Lord's input with every decision we make. We move forward on prayer, not impulse, and because we have surrendered, we are sheltered, and the path is clear.

There are four owners in our business now: Link and me, and my sister Dawn and her husband. We all know and love the Lord, and we seek His wisdom in all decisions. God has opened doors and He has closed them. We can see that it was not our responsibility to determine the course, but it was our responsibility to continue the momentum. Now the Lord has put others in charge of keeping this business in motion. This blessing means I can take care of my family. I can take care of Kaylee and homeschool our adopted son. I have time to write this book and give glory to God through my story.

When we acknowledge that the Lord is our Potter and refines us by continually working on perfecting us, life gets easier. I don't mean to suggest there are no longer struggles in our life, but when we understand that we have a limited capability to handle difficulties, it removes pressure. We do the work and put in the effort, and then rely on God to do the rest. If it fails, then it did not align with the Lord's will. The only way we are guaranteed to fail completely is when we give up entirely or stubbornly push our agenda. God determines the path, but we need to be willing to follow.

God strengthens us to fulfill our purpose, just as the military trains their recruits. There is no high-ranking military official who knows the recruits as intimately as God knows us. God knows everything about us, even our thoughts. The Lord also knows what burdens we can handle and how to increase our potential through trials and tribulation. John 16:33 (NKJV) says, "In the world you will have tribulation." That verse in John also says that Jesus tells us this so we can have peace—peace in the knowledge that the Lord has overcome the world, and He is in control of everything.

God has a purpose for each of His children, and He knows everything about us. We are on this planet for God, and He created us for His mission because He has a plan. There is a reason you are living at this time, in this place. It is because you have a calling on your life. Are you listening? Are you ready to surrender to the Lord and follow the path He cuts for you?

Faith Lesson: God controls everything, and He has a plan and a purpose for all of His children, but we must be willing to surrender to His will.

Ranch Talk

Surrendering to God for our welfare can be difficult, especially if we rely strictly on instinct. Animals rely on instinct for survival, but it doesn't always serve them well. Just like animals, we often run from things that make us uncomfortable, not realizing those situations are for our benefit.

When we had a couple of calves that needed doctoring, we ran them down the alley and into a squeeze chute. They were sick and required medication, but they were wild and flighty, and escape was their greatest motivation. We got the first one doctored, and when we started to run the second calf in the chute, it lunged forward and tried to jump over the side to escape. The calf sprung forward and hit its back on the drop gate of the chute. It immediately collapsed because the calf had broken its back.

We were trying to help it, and we were doing what was best for the calf. However, the calf's unwillingness to surrender ended in tragedy. Many may argue the calves did not know we were trying to help them, but isn't that the same with God?

We have a limited view, and we never know what the Lord's plan is. But we know He is good, and He wants an abundant life for us. Therefore we can trust Him, and we must submit to His will knowing

He is doing what is best for us. The funny thing is that the blessings the Lord has planned for us are far above what we can imagine. We think paradise is lying on the beach at an island resort, but God sees it as owning the island. God's view is *always* better.

Prayer

Heavenly Father, I pray You would help me determine the purpose You have for me and identify the brilliant gifts You have given me. I pray You will help me be diligent in using my gifts to help others and honor You, Lord. Please keep me from unnecessary distractions allow my mind to be sharp, my heart pure, and my path straight. I want to live for You, Lord, and I desire to impact this world for Your glory. I pray these things in Jesus' name, amen.

Study

Look up and write out James 4:10. _____

_____

_____.

Now I wish I had some magic formula for determining God's purpose for each of us, some close-your-eyes-and-spin-three-times solution. But since it has taken me most of my life to feel like I know what purpose God has for me, it is safe to say I have no magic solution. There have always been two things I was sure of, though. Since my late twenties, I felt led to write a book and adopt a child. I knew both of these things would happen. I just wasn't sure when.

So how do you determine the purpose God has for your life? I am making no promises, but let's see if I can help you narrow it down somewhat.

We each have different influences and experiences that have shaped the person we are today, and every person who reads this book will be in a unique personal spot on the road of life. But throw all of that out the window for just a short time, and as you answer the next few questions, don't let doubt or finances or personal fears limit your answers.

If it is what God has in mind for you, then nothing can stand in the way.

Name something you like to do that comes natural for you.

_____

(Examples could be to write, teach, coach, paint etc.)

What do you think your spiritual gift is? _____

_____

_____

I think we all have some idea of our spiritual gift based on certain tendencies we have. For example, one of my sisters has a servant's heart. She is the person who thinks about cooking dinner for someone with a sick family member or taking care of an older person. It just comes naturally to her.

Read Romans 12:1–8.

Look back at your answers, and ask yourself these questions.

How do my gifts and abilities help me teach others about God's love? _____

_____

The book "The Power of Faithful Focus" also offers guidance on discovering your purpose.[40]

Remember we are not here for our gain. To live in God's will, we have to be a witness for Christ. That doesn't mean you need to sell everything you own and enter the mission field unless that is your calling. There are many parts to the body of Christ.

You don't walk into class the first day as a student at a university and say, "Okay, I am ready to be the professor." No, you determine what you want to do, take the necessary steps to enroll in the classes, and then you learn. To work for the Lord, you need to put some effort in, and you need to know God and understand the Word of God. That is a job requirement.

You don't need to go to seminary school to learn God's Word. You can start by attending church, but you can also read a daily devotional or download a Bible app to your phone. I read the daily devotional on the Bible Hub app on my phone. Be careful with what you watch or study to avoid false doctrine. To learn God's Word from a trusted source, read "faith statements" that outline their core beliefs. Don Stewart is a trusted source at www.educatingourworld.com. I also trust Jack Hibbs, Greg Laurie, Pat Lazovich, and Ray Comfort.

The most important thing to remember is to be mindful of what you are being taught. One of my favorite sayings is, "Rat poison is 99% good food, but the 1% that is poison will kill you."

Faith to Weather the Storms

Then they cry out to the Lord in their trouble,
And He brings them out of their distresses.
He calms the storm, So that its waves are still.
Psalm 107:28–29 NKJV

"We were in the pickup headed to the ER when she started into another seizure. Her body stiffened, and I could hear the familiar clicking noise as her teeth clamped down. Then there was no sound. 'She isn't breathing,' I said. I had a feeling of hopelessness, and I calmly repeated the phrase, 'She is not breathing.'"

Storms of Life

There are times in our lives when we wish we could stay below the deck of the ship with covers pulled over our heads. Periods in our life seem full of loss and heartache, and we are not confident how we will weather another day. Those are the days many people will pull God off the shelf and grab His hand to guide them through the storm. However, these are also times in life when people can harden their hearts if they don't get what they want or when an outcome is not what they think is best from their limited human view.

As our children's services business slowly grew, our endless hours of effort were not yielding a profitable crop. But we were making a difference in the lives of many kids. We had initially started the business to help children with developmental disabilities. However, God began to change our course to some degree as we morphed to include children in the foster care system.

Our initial calling was providing respite and life-skill services to families with special needs children. Respite is a service that gives family caregivers a brief break. But as God worked in our business, I became aware of a needed service no one had addressed yet.

When children lose placement in the foster care system, time in respite care is a typical protocol. A respite stay often occurs preceding a new home and without the child knowing about the move to a new family. Loss of placement can happen for various reasons, but a common one is the mental and emotional burnout of foster parents. In my opinion, the movie *Instant Family* is a relatively accurate account of the foster and adoption life. Older children in this situation have most likely experienced physical and emotional trauma, and in many cases, it is extreme abuse. Therefore, it is only logical for them to lash out.

People who open their homes up to foster or adopt children in need will often require assistance themselves. A short break does wonders for a person's mental and physical well-being. Many placements stay intact by addressing this need and providing respite. A move to another family is one less trauma on these children. I expanded on a planned respite idea, reached out to agencies with my vision, and suggested our business to provide the care.

If we did not have an employee available to work, I would step in and work for free. As a Christian and a human being, how can I not do that? Link and I brought a three-year-old child into our home for three weeks while the state sought placement. No, we did not get paid for that. We took her in personally under kinship care.

It was a difficult three weeks because the state forbid me from telling her she had lost placement in her foster home. This tiny girl had experienced more trauma in her short three years of life than most experience in a lifetime. She cried every night because she wanted to go home, and I could tell her nothing. Fighting against the system was maddening.

I think she may have thought I had kidnapped her. The state placed her with a relative and shipped her off. It wasn't long before she stood abandoned on a street corner for the second time in her life. It is a broken system. Thankfully, the story had a happy ending for this little girl, and she is in a good home now.

As a company, we sometimes had to provide the services for free. We had to, not only because we felt called to do that, but because these kids needed us. One child was a young boy with special needs whose caregiver had gone into the hospital and died. We kept him for over a week after the state stopped paying. As an overnight facility, we gave him a place to live for almost a month.

Link and I were barely scraping by financially. I was driving a piece of junk around, and it was not incognito since I had a squeaking belt and brakes. I was embarrassed when my phone got disconnected because we were unable to pay the bill. It doesn't build a massive amount of confidence in your employees when the boss is barely scraping by. However, the employees always got paid, but I did not. I felt defeated, and I wanted to give up. Owning a business was hard, and I didn't know if I had what it took to stay in the fight. I was becoming very bitter and fought feelings of depression. No one envied my position or my pay.

Hatred for business owners is the disconnect our society has created around capitalism. Most people only see success when and if a capitalist becomes successful. No one sees or remembers the hardships—the blood, sweat, and tears it takes to build a business. We went without, and one year I had to ask my mom to loan me money so Taylor could have new school clothes. There were no vacations or new vehicles. My clothes came from a second-hand store, and Christmas came from the discount store. However, God provided everything we needed, including the will to continue.

When we were just about to go under again, God blessed Link with an opportunity to make some good money, and he jumped at the chance. It was a contracted welding job that would only last a few months, but the pay was phenomenal. He would be away from home again, but this opportunity was too good to pass up and had come along at just the right time.

Link would be earning a year's wages in three months. It was a much-needed miracle for us. God had swooped in and helped us again. Although I realize He had never left our side, this was the breath of air we needed. It filled the sails of our ship and kept us moving forward. I was so relieved and thankful.

We are never promised a life without trouble. It is, in fact, the opposite. The picture of a parent with a toddler who is just starting to walk comes to my mind. The Lord is the perfect Parent, and He walks behind us with His hand on either side. God doesn't want us to fall, and He is ready to catch us if we stumble. When we inevitably get some bumps, bruises, or scrapes, God is prepared to doctor and heal our wounds. Because we have free will to make our own decisions, some injuries are more profound than others. But we cannot expect to walk through life in a broken world shielded from every hurt. Since death is a natural part of life, we will also experience that.

God is faithful, and He heals our wounds and heartaches if we trust Him. The pain may never go away completely, especially when it involves death. But Christians have a promise from the Lord to be reunited with our loved ones who died in Christ. That is part of our blessed hope. Life is full of rough seas and storms because we live in a broken world. We didn't know it at this time, but there was a storm brewing on the horizon.

The year 2011 started with choppy seas when one of our pregnant family members received devastating news. Close to her due date, the doctor determined the baby was stillborn. A short time later, we received the news that one of my cousins had died in a house fire. The shock was unimaginable. I would never see him on this earth again. But time marches on regardless of our loss, and we must continue the course on which God has placed us.

In the previous six months, Link and I had started looking into adoption. Since we had a business based around children in the foster system, a friend had reached out to us for support and advice on her nephews. Her youngest brother had three boys in the foster care system, and his wife was expecting to deliver another child in March. Our friend was reaching out for advice on the two older boys. The state had removed the boys from a dangerous situation involving drugs. The parents were in and out of jail, and they skirted the system by fulfilling the state's minimum requirements. If they were supposed to attend counseling four times a month, they would go once. This system led to a perpetually open case and no permanent placement for the boys. We were new to this game and didn't realize how complicated the process would be. A third boy lived with an aunt, and there was a fourth child getting ready to be born into this chaotic mess.

I had always felt that God had placed a calling on my life for adoption, and I started the conversation with Link. We both agreed that we would pursue our foster care license and see if we could provide a home for these two boys.

We began taking a foster care licensing class in Tucson and preparing our home for licensing. The process was a struggle, and we were concerned about the state pushing to place the boys back with the mother and father, but we stayed the course.

We had the boys come and stay a few weekends and even took them to a family gathering.

It was a short two weeks after the family gathering when my mom started having issues with her stomach and was admitted to the hospital. Little did I know, Mom's cancer was back. My sisters knew this, but they had failed to inform me.

Since I had been fighting medical battles for Kaylee, I had grown bolder in the fight. I wanted everything for my mom, and when she needed something, I was not afraid to ask. On this particular day, the nurses seemed to have stopped responding to our requests, so I went on the hunt for my oldest sister, Gwen. When I found her talking to the doctors outside, I joined in to listen to the conversation. Dealing with hospitals and doctors had been a part of my life for over ten years now.

When I entered the conversation, I was still unaware of the gravity of the situation. Listening to what the doctor was saying, the realization started to sink in. I was unsure of what I had heard, but when I saw the look on my sister's face, I knew we were getting ready to lose our mom.

I tried to pull it together and went back to Mom's room. Her best friend, Carmen, was by her side, and when I looked at my mom, I couldn't hold the tears back. "Oh, don't cry," she said. I can still hear her saying that, and I can still hear her voice. She was strong even as she lay in a hospital bed, and how blessed she was to have a friend who would rush to her side.

When we drove home that night, God spoke to me through a song. "Praise You In This Storm" by Casting Crowns came on the radio. We are going to have troubles in this life on earth. We are going to experience trials and tribulation. We will experience the loss of loved ones, and we are going to die ourselves, eventually. That is the promise of this fallen world. The promise of God is a trouble-free eternity in heaven.

Sitting in the dark on the pickup's passenger side, I reached up to scratch my eyebrow. When I felt something crusty, I pulled it off, thinking about everyone I had seen that day. I looked over at Link. "You let me go the whole day with a booger on my eyebrow?" I couldn't believe he hadn't said anything to me. I had a booger on my eyebrow! I am not even sure how I got a booger on my eyebrow. Now I have always been convinced that God has a sense of humor. If God did not have a sense of humor, why would He give us one? When weathering the storms of life, we need to remember there can be humor amidst the clouds and laughter in the rain.

The next day my mom went to a hospice care facility, and as the family gathered, we knew our time with her was short.

On March 30, we received news that another baby boy had entered the world—born into the chaos surrounding the other three children in a broken family. His biological mother had not given him a name, but he was here, nonetheless.

On that same day, Mom passed away. We had gone to the hospice facility to tell her goodbye, and she was still breathing but unresponsive. We gathered around her bed, and it was peaceful as she departed this earth. Mom went into the emergency room with a stomach ache, and nine days later, she passed away.

Great-Uncle Alvin was devastated at the loss of my mom, and sadly he passed away shortly after Mom. Then one of my cousins lost her husband when he passed away in his sleep.

A few weeks later, my niece lost her fiancé in a tragic ranching accident two weeks before her wedding, and it seemed like more than we as a family could bear. When my sister called to tell me, I remember asking her, "What is happening?"

The final loss that year was when my mom's friend Carmen lost one of her sons. In seven short months, we had seven deaths in our family. The loss left our hearts broken, but we moved forward with thanksgiving on a blessed hope from God. We moved forward with the knowledge that we will see them in heaven.

Disappointment and loss are a part of life. In the book of Job, we read about significant loss. Job lost everything, including his children and his health. He was devastated and had to suffer his loss during a time of tremendous physical pain. I pray that I never have to go through a fraction of the tribulation that Job overcame. After the Lord spoke to Job, he answered and said, "I know that You can do everything, And that no purpose *of Yours* can be withheld from You" (Job 42:2 NKJV). God has a purpose and plan for every person, and

His timing determines our course in life.

Link and I put the adoption process on hold. When the state wanted to continue to pursue reunification with the father, we decided to back off on adopting the older boys. We did not want to be another home that the state would force them to leave. We felt at peace with this decision and open to God's plan.

In August of that year, we also had a scare with Kaylee. She had not had a seizure in over a year. Then without warning, she began convulsing. This episode was different because she was vomiting during the spasms. Her clenched jaw made me afraid she was going to choke on her vomit. Link grabbed medication to stop the seizure and administered the dose to her, and it did its job and stopped the seizure. Her body started to relax and as is usual for her, she was exhausted and wanted to sleep. However, a few minutes later, she started convulsing and vomiting again, which was not typical. Link gave her another dose of the medication, and the spasms stopped a second time. Since she had never had two seizures consecutively, Link picked her up and carried her to the pickup.

Taylor and I gathered some things and jumped in the pickup. I got in the back seat with Kaylee, who at this point remained non-responsive. We were in the pickup headed to the ER when she started into another seizure. Her body stiffened, and I could hear the familiar clicking noise as her teeth clamped down. Then there was no sound. "She isn't breathing," I said. I had a feeling of hopelessness, and I calmly repeated the phrase, "She is not breathing." The continual seizures left me depleted and removed every ounce of panic in me. I felt helpless.

Kaylee spent three days in intensive care, and they determined there was another active seizure area in her brain. They put her on a second medication, and thank God, she has not had a seizure for over nine years.

Afterthought

As believers in Christ, our faith got tested that year in a dramatic way. It is easy to be a fair-weather believer. However, I could never imagine not having the Lord in our times of trouble. God is the only One who can instill hope, and the Lord is the only One in control. It is easy to throw a tantrum when we don't get our way, but standing firm in faith is the only thing that heals the heart. That doesn't mean we do not grieve or feel sad, but we do so with trust in the Lord. We grieve with hope in a joyful promise from God.

The tough times come to everyone. Loss may not look the same on the surface, but it is still devastating. Losing so many loved ones in quick succession was a hard blow for our family. People who go through trials like this without the Lord tend to become bitter. They harden their hearts and look at life through scratched lenses. But no one is immune to death; it comes to everyone. Therefore, it is crucial to count the blessings and not the scars. When we count our scars, we look at the pain of the past, not the hope of the future.

God does not want a fair-weather friend. If we know that we can count on the Lord when the clouds cover the sky and the lightning strikes from east to west, why would we not share the sun-filled days with Him as well? We should delight in the Lord just as He delights in us. God is with us every day. He delights in our company, and we should rejoice in His presence.

That year was by far the most challenging our family has faced. With loss so profound and in quick succession, we could hardly catch our breath. However, we did find humor in the storm at times. When we gathered around Mom's bed on her last day, someone said, "I bet Mom is saying, 'Why are you all standing around staring at me?'" and that made us chuckle. We found laughter in the rain when we retold stories and remembered Mom as we went through her belongings. There were tears and laughter and joy and pain.

We all face disappointment and loss in life. That is part of our portion in this fallen world, but as Christians, we need to remember this world is not our home.

Faith Lesson: God is faithful to never leave our side. He holds our hand when we are lost, and carries us when we are broken.

Ranch Talk

One year we had a cattle buyer who sold the fall calf crop to John Wayne. We were all very excited at the prospect of meeting the famous actor. The buyer said that John would come to the ranch when we loaded the trucks to ship the calves out. It was a big day, and we were even going to miss school to meet "the Duke."

My mom could hardly wait, and she stepped away from cooking to sneak a peek. She didn't want to get in the way or be seen, so she crept up to the fence unnoticed. As she slowly climbed up the fence to peek over the top rail, she was sorely disappointed. Sitting on the top rail on the other side of the corral was not a famous actor. John had sent his business partner to oversee the purchase of our calves. We were all disappointed, but at least we kids got a day off of school.

My mom told the cattle buyer that he was nothing but a "bull-shipper," and I am not sure if he thought that was funny, but we did. My sister Laura remembers Mom saying that she was so mad she felt she had over-kneaded the bread, but it was the best bread she had ever made.

Life is full of disappointment and loss. That was a funny story told for years after the fact, but most of life's letdowns are not so humorous. However, when people experience difficulty without hope, they can become indignant. The saved grieve differently from the unsaved. People with no hope have lost someone forever, but those with blessed hope know they will see their loved one again.

Some mistakenly believe they can rail against God and harbor a grudge because they will have a second chance. They are so mired down in bitterness that their pride will not allow them to surrender and receive forgiveness. You cannot "plead your case" when you stand before the Lord. The decision we as humans make today will affect our lives for eternity. Greg Laurie often reminds us that all paths will lead to God because every person will stand before Him in judgment. However, not all routes will lead to heaven. There is only one way to heaven, and that is through Jesus and His sacrifice on the cross.

Prayer

Heavenly Father, I pray for those who remain lost in grief. They are bitter because they do not have hope, and they are allowing their pride to keep them from Your blessings and protection. I pray for those who continue to fight against You, Lord, and I pray they realize they are keeping themselves from Your promises and hope. I am so thankful that I know You, Father, and that my faith is in You. I pray for Your continued shelter as I face the storms of this life. In Jesus' name, amen.

Study

Look up and write down 2 Peter 1:10. _____

_____

_____

_____

I thought back to try and determine possible barriers I should have removed before attempting to discern God's purpose for my life. While I cannot promise you will know precisely the purpose God has for you, I'm hoping that by the end of the book, you will at least be closer to that discovery.

Revelation 3:8 (NLT) says, "I know all the things you do, and I have opened a door for you that no one can close. You have little strength, yet you obeyed my word and did not deny me." The Lord has opened the door for you because He has a plan for your life. No one can snatch the plan God has for our lives.

The apostle Peter said we need to make every effort to add these attributes to our lives. However, notice that you need to add these qualities to the faith you should already possess, because our belief comes when we accept Christ as our Savior.

List out the qualities mentioned in 2 Peter 1:5–7 (NKJV). _____

_____ , _____

_____ , _____

, _____ , _____

_____ , _____

_____ , _____ .

In 2 Peter 1:8, we are told we not only need to have these qualities, but we also need to increase them. Every day we are supposed to grow as Christians, and in return, these qualities will grow. To bear fruit in our lives, we must be productive and effective in our knowledge of our Lord Jesus Christ. It is essential to spend time with the Lord every day.

I believe our company is successful because we have focused on the kids and not the money. If you hope to fulfill the purpose God has, then your heart's desire has to align with the Lord's will—with what matters to Him. I am not saying that God wants you to remain broke or broken, because look at Job. God restored everything in his life to more than he had before the trial.

If I had done the exercise in the previous chapter, these are the results I would have written down. I am going to show my examples so this can possibly help you finetune your answers.

Talent or Ability: _Write, Organize Events_____

_____

How would this serve God? _Helps others, a way to teach others about God, a way to serve the Lord, or a way to give._

Spiritual Gift: _Teaching_____

How would this serve God? _Volunteer or have a Bible Study_

Now, let's apply the qualities from above and see what we might learn from my example as it pertains to writing this book.

A definition of **virtue** is the conformity of one's life and conduct to moral and ethical principles. No one will ever be perfect, and we cannot change our past. We must strive every day to be better, and the only way we can do that is through the Lord.

Virtue: <u>Cover my day in prayer that the words of my mouth and my actions will be pleasing to the Lord.</u>

Knowledge: <u>Study God's Word daily through devotions, Bible studies, etc.</u>

Self-control: <u>To think before I act, recognize when I falter, and cover it in prayer.</u>

Perseverance: <u>Do not give up. If I hit a closed door, pray and keep moving, and realize I may have to change course. This is God's plan not mine.</u>

The definition of **godliness** from the Webster dictionary is "careful observance of, or conformity to, the laws of God."[41] Unlike the definition from some religions, this does not mean becoming a god. We are not called to be gods or promised that in the Bible.

Godliness: <u>Submit to the Lord's will in my life and surrender my life to Him.</u>

Mutual affection: <u>Have compassion for my fellow human beings and remember that we have all sinned and fall short of the glory that is God's alone.</u>

Love: <u>Set aside my pride and love others as I love myself. Change my heart and the way I think about others. To know God is to know how to love.</u>

Look back at your answers from the previous chapter and write them below. These should be the revised answers that serve God.

Talent or Ability: _____

How to serve God: _____

Spiritual Gift: _____

How to serve God: _____

Now create your action plan around the seven qualities we are called to possess. This process will revolve around a strategy to grow in each area of your life personally. We are called to bear fruit, and to do that, we need to strengthen our root systems and become healthy Christians.

Virtue: _____
_____

Knowledge: _____
_____

Self-control: _____
_____

Perseverance: _____
_____

Godliness: _____
_____

Mutual affection: _____
_____

Love: _____
_____

Faith from Ashes

*God blesses those who patiently endure testing and
temptation. Afterward they will receive the crown of
life that God has promised to those who love him.*
James 1:12 NLT

"When the text came through, I looked at my phone, and my
heart dropped. The text read, 'Kaylee broke her right hip.' I
fought back the feeling of panic, reminding myself that God was in
control."

Regeneration

Life can be like a fire. Things can feel under control, then the
blaze gets out of hand and devastation sweeps through. We light a
match in every decision we make, and when we strike without seeking God's will, the flame can either burn out or blaze in destruction.
When the world has burned around you and you stand in a pile of
ashes, either your faith will wither or it will bloom. When faith is
allowed to wither and die, the choice is made not to accept God's will

in our lives. When faith blooms from the ashes, we can say with confidence, "Your will be done, Lord." Accepting the will of God in our lives can seem scary at times. After all, we always think we know best. However, when we trust that God knows best, our blessings will flow. Our lives regenerate with our faith restored by trusting in the Lord.

As we put the year of loss behind us, things began to change. It wasn't easy without our mom, and our dad took the loss extremely hard.

We began to experience "the firsts" in life after loss. The first Thanksgiving without Mom was challenging. There was a large hole in a family that centered life around Mom and Dad. Thanksgiving in 2011, we went to my sister Laura's house, and it wasn't until we were all there cooking when we realized we would have our first Thanksgiving without cranberries. Mom always made them, and we had completely forgotten to include the dish in our planning.

Laura's husband worked on a large ranch in New Mexico at the time, so we were literally in the middle of nowhere. There were no neighbors for miles, so we knew we had a Thanksgiving blessing when their friends stopped by and delivered a dish of, you guessed it, cranberries. God speaks to us and blesses us through other people.

As Christians, we look forward to our ultimate destination, but we should also enjoy the journey. There is beauty in every day when we live in the hope of the Lord.

For Link and me, our lives were also changing, and our trust in God was growing. With a leap of faith, we agreed to pursue a foster placement with the fourth baby boy, who was born the night before Mom passed away. There was already chaos and drama surrounding his life, but we boldly stepped into the battle. His biological mother had left a field of ashes as she burned every blessing in her self-centered pursuit for happiness. She had walked out of the hospital and left this helpless new soul without a name, suffering from drug withdrawal on a morphine drip.

Link and I both felt a strong calling from God to step in and offer this baby a home and a family. Our first interaction with the birth mother was at a child service meeting. She was looking to give him to her "friends" to raise. I sat and looked at an older man in his late 70s with his older daughter and wondered why they wanted to raise another child. In light of the recent discoveries on child trafficking, I can't help but wonder if they sat in that meeting driven by money. A helpless child with no name would be a prime victim.[42]

The case manager looked at the birth mother and said, "Well, Beth, you haven't named him yet. Do you know what his name will be?"

Beth looked at the woman she had brought to the meeting with her and asked, "What would you like to name him?"

Pompously the woman stated, "I would like to name him Raul, after my father."

One of the aunts on the birth father's side sharply stated, "We are not calling him Raul because we have named him Collin."

Link and I followed the conversation like a tennis match as the dialog and anger continued. The baby was only ten days old, and chaos surrounded his life. A determination that the baby would reside with the birth father's sister and one of his older brothers made it seem finished. However, when God has a plan, no one can change it. No one can close a door that God opens. Six months later, Collin came to live with us. We anxiously accepted a new baby into our lives and our home. There were still some hard roads ahead; however, we were willing to go through the door God had opened.

God works all things for our good, but we need to be willing to go through the fire to receive the blessing. Dealing with the foster care system and the biological parents was frustrating as the state continued to push reunification with the birth parents. However, there was light at the end of the tunnel.

No matter what we dealt with, life around us marched on and

in 2012, we had a wedding. Taylor found a young cowboy and fell in love. Link had a tough time letting go of his daughter, and it took some adjusting, but he was finally happy about the addition of a son-in-law. I am proud of the young woman we raised and the love and trust she has in the Lord. Her new husband accepted Jesus while they were dating. Our family was growing, and the blessings of the Lord were abundant.

The business we had started years before was also flourishing, and Link quit his construction job as a blade operator and became the CEO of our company. However, we acknowledged that God was the actual CEO, which is what blessed our business. It was by the Lord's hand that we kept our doors open and grew the way we did. God blessed every meeting, project, and service. With our partners, we covered everything in prayer. If there was a meeting with the state or a business we contracted with, God oversaw every aspect. We have been diligent in giving God the glory because He is the only reason for our success.

In 2013, we were ecstatic to welcome our first grandson, Kail, and in 2016, we were blessed again with our granddaughter Kadence. Time marched on, and for the most part, life remained steady and calm. However, my dad continued to struggle and took a sharp turn for the worse when he was helping my sister feed her livestock—and his femur snapped.

The consequences of the surgery were devastating as he struggled with the aftereffects of anesthesia. He combated sundowners, and his memory sharply declined. When he complained of pain and struggled with regaining his mobility, it was discovered that the surgeon had botched the initial procedure, and he would need additional surgery. We had to move him into an assisted living facility as we watched him continue to decline. But even when we face profound challenges, we cannot push a pause button; life continues to march on.

When Kaylee graduated from high school, we were thankful one of the boys in her class agreed to walk with her during the ceremony. Since we wanted her to have some semblance of a typical life, we started looking for an assisted living home for her. We were excited when we found a place, but I was nervous about her care. I felt the Lord had brought us to this house when I looked at the wall and saw Proverbs 3:5 (NKJV), "Trust in the Lord with all your heart, And lean not on your own understanding."

I trusted that the Lord had led us to this home, and I had to trust Him to protect her. Once we moved her in, I quickly learned to pick my battles. After all, did it really matter if she had a bath at night instead of in the morning?

In May of 2019, we welcomed another grandbaby into the family with our grandson Karson. Other than the difficulties with my dad, life had been smooth sailing, and we felt God's protection over us.

In August, I felt convicted by the message at church. The youth pastor was filling in, and he talked about the junk we watch on television. His family had decided to subscribe to a TV network, and two days later, they canceled their service.

After we left the church service, I discovered that Link was as convicted as I was, so we decided to fast from network television for one month. We went from watching several hours of our favorite shows every evening to wondering what to do with that time. We started buying Christian videos beginning with creation and then expanded from there. When the month was up, we did not reconnect our network television.

We had started down the road of discovering more about God and couldn't get enough. We watched everything dealing with creation to the book of Revelation and everything in between that covered the pages of the Bible. As our knowledge increased, so did our outreach. Our lives were changing drastically, and so was our outlook. I was excited to share everything I was learning. When we opted for television again, we went to a streaming service, but we did not go back to watching our old shows. We continued in our pursuit of God. We began watching Greg Laurie, Jack Hibbs, Ray Comfort, and Don Stewart.

Growing continually in God's Word helped me deal better with the difficulties surrounding my dad. Doctors had diagnosed him with Alzheimer's, and he steadily declined. We moved him from an assisted living facility to an assisted living home. He still had his own bedroom, but he had someone reminding him to eat, unlike at the facility. Alzheimer's steals so much from both the victim and their family. It is immensely challenging when your own dad does not know who you are. I walked into his room one day, and he thought I was a therapist. When I took him for a drive, he asked several times who I was. It was at this point when I realized how much God had changed me. When I could smile and patiently answer the same question with the same answer over and over, I knew I had grown in the Lord. Growth in God's Word is the only weapon we have in the battle we call life.

At the close of 2019, I had no clue what was on the horizon. On Christmas Eve, I prepared for Link's family to come for dinner. I felt tired, and I was operating out of sheer will to get my house cleaned and ready to host our guests. I slow-roast my turkey for Christmas Day, so after our guests left on Christmas Eve, I started the turkey and then collapsed in bed. When I woke up at 2:30 a.m. to check on the turkey, I did not feel well.

I climbed back in bed, and the chills that shook my body woke Link up. I could not stop shaking. I typically get up extra early on Christmas morning, but this year was different as I could barely summon the energy to sit up in bed. I was sick on Christmas Day.

I forced myself to get up to open presents and watch my family open their gifts, but went right back to my bed when we finished. I ached all over, and on the evening of the day after Christmas, Link took me to the emergency room. I was reluctant to go. Past trips to the ER left me skeptical, and I lacked confidence in our town's hospital. However, I could no longer stand the pain, and I was having difficulty breathing.

The physician entered the room and said, "You either have blood clots in your lungs or pneumonia." He ordered an x-ray and an MRI, and then with the test results, he came back in and said, "Congratulations, it's just pneumonia." I had contracted pneumonia for the first time.

A week later, Kaylee was sick. When one of the staff took Kaylee to the urgent care, I warned her about the possibility of pneumonia. I was so happy to find out that the staff stood their ground where Kaylee was concerned. They wanted to send her home, but the person who took her in insisted they test for pneumonia. Kaylee also had contracted pneumonia, and the year 2020 was off to a rocky start.

At the end of January, I received a call from one of Kaylee's caregivers. She told me that Kaylee had been targeted by a young man who had an outburst at the day program. He had kicked her leg out from underneath her. Kaylee is only twenty-one, but she unfortunately has the body of an eighty-year-old.

They asked if I wanted the ambulance to take her to the emergency room, and I insisted they do that. Since Kaylee could not articulate the actual pain point, they took x-rays of her knee and ankle and sent her home. Kaylee has a history of overdramatizing things, especially when people baby her. I wasn't worried because she had seen a doctor, and they had taken x-rays. However, when they told me three days later that she threw herself to the ground in a fit, I became concerned. Kaylee is physically unable to throw herself to the ground. She is both too stiff and too cautious. Since I tend to process information slowly, it didn't hit me until one o'clock that next morning. I sat up in bed and thought, *It's her hip.*

I insisted they take her back to the ER and x-ray her hip, and then I began the waiting game. Had she spent three days trying to get around with a broken hip? With her high pain tolerance, it wouldn't surprise me.

I was still stunned when I received the text. The fall had broken Kaylee's left hip, and they would be admitting her for surgery. That fire was blazing now, and my mind reeled in a state of both panic and guilt.

The fracture was at the neck of her femur. The added trauma of her attempts to walk had increased the separation between the ball and the femur. Kaylee needed major surgery. It took over a week in the hospital before we brought her home.

During the hospital days, I started to let my mind get ahead of God and anticipate all of the worst-case scenarios. The thoughts stressed me out, and I became increasingly short-tempered. When a case manager came in to tell me there was no possibility of getting a home health nurse, I could take no more. I did not yell at her, but I was not pleasant, and when she left the room, I felt immediately convicted. It was not her fault, and I knew I needed to apologize.

Her office was a cubical in the unit and just down the hall from Kaylee's room. I got her attention as I walked up. "I wanted to apologize for losing my peace," I said. "I am feeling very frustrated over this whole situation, and I know it is not your fault." My voice cracked as I said the words, and tears began to stream down my face. The storm of emotions I had suppressed surfaced, and when she thanked me for the apology, I left.

As I walked away, I fought to hold back the overwhelming emotion. My stress and fear were bubbling to the surface when a thought came to mind: *Don't get ahead of God.*

At that moment, I realized that all of the thoughts swirling around in my brain were *what-if* thoughts. *What if* the incision gets infected? *What if* she can't walk after this? They were endless. However, the biggest question I needed to ask myself was, "*What if* none of these issues occur?" I was creating problems before they ever came to light, and by doing that, I was living in the future.

Matthew 6:34 (NLT) says, "So don't worry about tomorrow, for tomorrow will bring its own worries. Today's trouble is enough for today." We are told not to live in the future because we do not know what it holds. I was getting ahead of God and creating scenarios that were affecting my mental well-being. To combat this, I had to recognize the Enemy was leading me down that path and remind myself, "Don't get ahead of God."

Because I was willing to humble myself and apologize to the case manager, she became a valuable advocate. She helped me navigate the system, and we were able to get a home health nurse and two therapists for in-home care. When I wheeled Kaylee out of the hospital a couple of days later, I felt at peace. I knew we might face some challenges, but I also knew God was in control.

The Bible reveals God's control in all of its books. One such example is in Isaiah 38, when God sends the prophet Isaiah to tell King Hezekiah that he will die. Hezekiah had become ill, and Isaiah told him that the Lord said he needed to put his house in order and prepare for his death. The king did not turn to anyone but the Lord, and he prayed and cried out to God. Hezekiah humbled himself and wept bitterly and said, "'Remember, O Lord, how I have always been faithful to you and have served you single-mindedly, always doing what pleases you.' Then he broke down and wept bitterly" (Isaiah 38:3 NLT).

God heard Hezekiah's prayers and saw his tears, and he sent Isaiah back to tell the king he would let him live fifteen more years. Isaiah 38:4 (NKJV) says, "And the word of the Lord came to Isaiah, saying. . . " So God speaks to us through thoughts and words from other people. When Hezekiah cried out to the only One who could help him, God heard his plea and answered him through Isaiah. We need to humble ourselves and cry out to God.

Kaylee recovered well, and we did not face any of the issues that had been swirling around in my thoughts. In March, when the world shut down due to Covid-19, we decided to keep her home. She was still receiving therapy at home and was beginning to get around without her walker. She had a bone density test, and the results were not encouraging as we found she had osteoporosis.

When Easter came, Dad became gravely ill, and things were not looking good for him. We knew we needed to say our good-byes. Thankfully, God had intervened in his life. The lady who had been spending time with him moved him into her home when the lockdowns started, so it was a blessing he could still have visitors. However, the night before I planned to go up, Kaylee ran a fever of 104°, and I could not see him. Dad passed away before I could say goodbye to him, but thankfully, I am confident I will see him again.

As we moved into the early months of summer, Kaylee was mobile and healthy, so we decided to let her move back to her assisted living home. They were still locked down, but she would be around her other housemates, and we thought she might be happier.

It was around this time when I was scrolling on social media that an advertisement for an online writing conference popped up on my feed. I had given up on my dream of writing a book years ago, but I was intrigued and talked to Link about spending the money. Since I have a very supportive husband, he encouraged me to attend.

Kaylee's transition back to the home was simple since we had not moved any of her things out. However, three weeks later, tragedy struck again. When I received another call from a staff member at the assisted living home, I answered it unprepared. She told me that Kaylee had gone to sit down in her chair and fell again.

The staff member said that Kaylee was still in a good mood and laughing and joking around, so I was not overly concerned but wanted her taken to the ER.

When the text came through, I looked at my phone, and my heart dropped. The text read, "Kaylee broke her right hip." I fought back the feeling of panic, reminding myself that God was in control. But I could hardly believe it. We were facing another surgery, and it had only been a little over four months since the last incident. We had attempted to step through a door that God did not open, and we were back at square one.

I stayed home with Collin as Link drove the hour to the emergency room. We knew we wanted her moved to a different hospital because we wanted her to have her second surgery in the same place as her first one. The ER doctor was not pleased and informed Link that they would process the transfer, but they refused to transport her to the other hospital.

In an attempt to suppress the panic, I continued to repeat the phrase, "Don't get ahead of God. He holds it in His hands." The *what-if* questions were swirling at a dizzying pace. However, God did not abandon us because He is faithful. When my phone rang, I instinctively answered even though I did not recognize the incoming number. I was surprised when I realized it was the surgeon who had performed Kaylee's first hip surgery in January.

I was amazed again by how God works. What are the chances of a top surgeon in a large hospital looking at a transfer form and personally reaching out to a patient? This surgeon had seen Kaylee only a handful of times, and I was amazed he had recognized her name and called to see what had happened. In my opinion, that was none other than God.

Since I have faith that God has a hand in everything that happens, and the Bible tells us this is the case. I believe God did this. Link said the hospital had everything ready for Kaylee's arrival when he got there. She had surgery on Sunday, and I drove her home on Tuesday. Two days in the hospital was amazing to me, and Kaylee was ready to get out of there, so she was motivated to get up.

Link and I both concluded that God wanted Kaylee in our home. We have no idea what the Lord is protecting her from, but we are confident she is where He wants her. Two broken hips in a little over four months is a pretty good sign, and we obeyed.

In August of that year, our lives changed in several ways. Because we did not want to send Collin back to school due to Covid-19 and the mask situation, I became a homeschool teacher. At fifty-one years old, I decided to take on the challenge of educating our son. I had thought about this for several years because of the decline in the public school curriculum, but I had let doubt stop me.

Collin had been struggling with learning. When he was in kindergarten, he had eye surgery; however, that improved his ability very little, so I sought other solutions. When I found a developmental optometrist, he received real results with therapy and glasses. Unfortunately, his schoolwork was still lacking, and we were encouraged to place him in special education and develop an IEP, which we did. Because of these added problems, I was afraid I would fail him through homeschooling, but God had other plans.

We never know what the future will bring, but we can always have faith that God controls everything. The apostles told us to look for Jesus' return and to prepare.

The casting of this world into chaos is a reality, and in less than a year, everything changed dramatically and is all unrecognizable. It is easy to find ourselves mourning over our losses, but that is an earthly view. I wholeheartedly admit I am among the guilty; however, I have to remind myself that I need a heavenly perspective. No one knows the day or the hour that Christ will return, but today is one day closer.

Afterthought

When that blaze gets out of control, it can feel like a fire has swept through and decimated our life. However, fire is also a regenerating force in nature. The Forest Service and ranchers have used fire to regenerate land for well over a century.[43] The ashes from the burned plants return nutrients to the soil quicker than decomposition, and the fire destroys harmful insects. The regeneration of plants after a fire is magnificent, and everything grows back healthier.

None of us knows what the future holds. The events of 2020 should remind us that we have no control over the things that happen. We need to accept God's will, because He knows what is best for each of us. The Lord determines which doors to shut and which to open.

The world around us preaches self-sufficiency and tries to instill the notion that accepting help is a sign of weakness. But, when we welcome assistance from the One who holds everything in His hands, we are stronger than anything around us. Nothing can stand against God, and nothing will fail when we live according to His will. The Bible tells us that God opens and closes doors in our lives (Revelation 3:7–8). If we are knocking on a door that the Lord has shut, we are knocking in vain.

After I finished the writing conference and attended another seminar, I signed a contract to write my book. I had been diligently in God's Word for almost a year, and it was finally time. God opened the door for me to write my story. In a year when it felt as if God had closed the door for the world, He was actually opening our eyes.

We welcomed another grandson, Kole, in January 2021, and I am also happy to report that Collin has made tremendous progress through homeschooling. His handwriting, math, and reading skills have improved because of the one-on-one attention. Kaylee has recovered well and is still living at home with us and in January of 2021, geneticists finally determined she has DYRK1A syndrome. Taylor, her husband, Wyatt, and our grandkids are doing great. Wyatt oversees part of a large ranch so my grandkids are growing up in that life too.

Link and I celebrated our thirty-first anniversary in 2020, and our marriage has never been stronger. We have grown in the Lord together, and His love and blessings on our life have been tremendous.

I don't know what the future holds, but God knows. In 2020, the Lord took the focus off worldly pleasures and directed the world to view matters of real importance. When our lives became devoid of movies, sports, and restaurants, we opened our eyes. We looked up and saw a bigger picture. We see a world full of sin and false doctrine, but we should also see a world full of opportunity.

As Christians, we need to keep our eyes open and look up to the heavens. We are living in an exciting time as our stay on earth is near its end. Can you imagine how awesome it would be to be caught up in the air in the blink of an eye?

Matthew 6:19 (NKJV) says, "Do not lay up for yourselves treasures on earth, where moth and rust destroy and where thieves break in and steal." Earthly treasures are temporary and will eventually decay. When we get caught up in material objects, they become our focus in life, but the happiness we acquire from these things is fleeting. The things on this earth will eventually decay, that diamond ring and the new car will lose their luster, and to obtain more happiness, we must buy more stuff. Matthew 6:21 says that our hearts are with our treasures.

When we care too much about this world's things, we are missing what is truly important. We will reside on this planet for a brief moment in time, but there will be an eternity with our heavenly treasures. Our heavenly treasures include our friends and loved ones because residing with them for eternity is part of that inheritance of the kingdom of God. There is no material object on this earth which we can carry with us to heaven. Only other souls can go along.

Therefore, where are you putting your effort? Are you working to obtain more stuff, or are you sharing the good news of salvation? We are the light of the world, so we must make sure that everyone sees that light. Everyone is welcome, but not all will come.

Faith Lesson: When we look for God's protection and intervention through the eyes of faith, we see it in every situation.

Ranch Talk

When things happen that we don't understand, we must trust there is a reason. We may never know the reason or the tragedy we may have avoided, but God knows.

Link and I were looking for a horse for Collin, and we found one we were very interested in trying. We brought him home, and even though he was older, we determined he may be too much horse for Collin.

I was excited to ride him. It had been several years since I had been on a horse, and I looked forward to riding again. When Link went to turn him out, he was feeling good, and when he started to whirl and buck his foot slipped, and he fell. He got up but was having a hard time walking, so Link called the vet.

Tragically, the fall had broken his leg, and the vet had to put him down. I was extremely disappointed and sad at the loss of this beautiful animal, but I wondered if God kept us from something. I will never know for sure.

We need to trust in God and understand that He keeps us safe. It is by the Lord's hand that I have escaped many tragedies in my life. I trust He protects me every day to live out my purpose on this earth.

Prayer

Thank You for the protection You give, Lord. Thank You for the armor of Your Word, which we must use to protect us. You are so faithful, God, and I give You the glory for everything in my life. As we move forward, I pray for Your continued guidance and shielding ,not only over myself but over my loved ones and this world. I trust You, Lord, and pray these things in Jesus' name, amen.

Study

I want to end this study with my favorite verse. Look up and write down Jeremiah 29:11. _____

_____

_____

It is written as a promise to the Israelites and based on a covenant God made with David.[44] This verse shows that our God keeps His promises because He knows what His plans are. God has a plan and a purpose for each of us. This promise means God is watching over you and cares about you. It does not mean God promises you a trouble-free life of luxury or wealth. But it does mean you have a calling on your life and a purpose.

However, when we search to find our purpose, it can be challenging. Pursuing God's will in our lives is pleasing to the Lord. When we concern ourselves with our heavenly Father's desire, we look to higher things and a higher plan.

The Lord has given us a Helper in the Holy Spirit and words of wisdom in the Bible. When we read and learn God's Word, we equip ourselves for the job ahead. Through prayer, we ask for wisdom and quiet ourselves to hear His voice. As we grow in God's Word and strive to be more Christlike, we set ourselves apart from others. We will never be perfect because that is impossible, but we shine a light in this dark world when we strive to be a better human being.

We must pursue holiness and live in God's Word. You have to know what the Bible says. It is a daunting task to sit down and read the Bible, but daily devotions and Bible studies are a great way to learn God's Word.

I recently participated in a twenty-one-day "Find Your Compass" challenge by Natalie Hodson.[45] The challenge was not a Christian course, but I gathered some valuable information, and she introduced me to an exciting concept. She encouraged us to set a daily goal of "good, better, and best." This practice works best when you post it in a visible spot; ideally, a dry erase board hanging on your wall.

"Good" is something you will do to keep momentum, typically the bare minimum, but still a win. Obviously, "better" is a step above, and "best" your ultimate goal.

Write your goals for growing in God's Word in the "good, better, best" format, and post them in a place you will see every day. It could look something like the following:

Good: Read one Bible verse a day.
Better: Read a devotional every day.
Best: Read a devotional daily and look up each verse.
Now it is your turn.

Good: _____

Better: _____

Best: _____

Remember: You don't have to be perfect you just need momentum.

Conclusion

The Gate Is Narrow

Our lives will continually change because nothing stays the same here in this fallen world. That is why we are told not to set our treasures upon earth but in heaven.

It is easy to get caught up in the things we enjoy in our lives on this planet. I am so guilty of this, and I must remind myself that nothing on this earth will matter when I am in heaven. Everything on this planet will decay and waste away. It will all burn in the end.

When we live as someone saved through Jesus, we know we are leaving something that is dying. We see the signs that this world is on the verge of burning, and we know we will be exiting to safety soon. If you were in the motion of leaving a physical structure that was on fire, would you walk out and let the party rage on upstairs? Would you let people burn up because you are afraid you will face ridicule?

There is no pleasure in ridicule. However, we must be able to stand before the Lord with a clear conscience. God calls us to be witnesses, and if we would not let people burn in a building, why would we let them burn at the end?

Witnessing is not easy, and false doctrine has diluted the words in the Bible. People falsely believe there are many roads to heaven.[46] False teachers want everyone to think they can create a form of god that pleases them. However, that type of message is what creates idols and sends people down a trail of darkness. Matthew 7:13–14 says that the gate is narrow and the path is straight that leads to life. Like Greg Laurie says, "All roads lead to God, but only one road leads to heaven."[47] Every human will stand before God in judgment, but not all will go to heaven.

The words in the Bible are without flaw and have stood the test of true prophecy. No one has rewritten the words in the Bible, and they fit with history perfectly. It is a book written in a span of 1500 years by approximately forty different authors, in three different languages, and across three different continents.[48] The Bible contains a unity in purpose, thought, and narrative, and projects truth that is undeniable. How can anyone deny the Bible is the Word of God?

I don't mean to offend anyone, but false doctrine denies the truth of the Bible. When told that people can create a personal version of god, or have multiple chances to achieve heaven, that is false doctrine. When people rewrite the Bible or add to the Word, that is also false doctrine.[49]

So how do we recognize false doctrine and false prophets? Deuteronomy 18:22 (NKJV) says, "When a prophet speaks in the name of the Lord, if the thing does not happen or come to pass, that *is* the thing which the Lord has not spoken; the prophet has spoken it presumptuously; you shall not be afraid of him." Every false religion has a prophet who has spoken words that did not come to pass. Every false religion has added to or taken away from the Bible's words, which is forbidden. There are various deflections and defenses for the words that man has added, but my question is, how do you know which one to believe? If you are learning doctrine from sources other than the Bible, how do you know you are following the right religion? If you say it is because you meditated and prayed about it to know that it was truth, you are still deceived. Every false religion tells people to meditate and pray before following it because man's heart is deceitful.

Any religion that discourages or forbids the reading of the Bible should send people running for the door. When attending a church that teaches the Bible's validity and infallibility, you are never forbidden from reading false doctrine because you have the armor of God's truth. There is no fear of false teachings when you know what the Bible says, because when you have certainty in God's Word, a lie cannot blind or bind you.

Religions steeped in falsehood discourage reading the Bible because they are afraid it will open people's eyes to facts they want to keep hidden. However, when taught to have a relationship with the Savior and not the church, and you know what the Word of God says, deception is impossible.

If your church has its own book, what do you have to lose by testing it against the Word of God? If it is true, it will stand, and if it is false doctrine, it will fall.[50] There is a problem if you know the book from your "religion" better than the Bible. It is our responsibility to be discerning, especially when it comes to where we will spend eternity.

Answer the following questions to get the biblical view of your religion.

The Bible tells us that hell is a real place, and the unrepentant will reside there in eternal torment (Revelation 20:15; 2 Thessalonians 1:8). Jesus talked about hell more than heaven, so to deny the existence of hell goes against the words of Jesus. Matthew 10:28 (NKJV) says, "And do not fear those who kill the body but cannot kill the soul. But rather fear Him who is able to destroy both soul and body in hell." Matthew 25:46 (NKJV) says, "And these will go away into everlasting punishment, but the righteous into eternal life." Look up what your book says about hell, outer darkness, or any punishment after death. Does it go along with what the Bible says?

The Bible says there is a narrow gate to heaven, and few will find it (Matthew 7:13–14). Many false religions teach there are multiple ways to get to heaven, and you will have a second chance after you die, but that is not accurate when tested against the Bible. If there are many roads to heaven, then why would Jesus suffer and die on the cross? God will destroy those who do not take the narrow path (Jeremiah 12:17), and He will save those who ask for salvation (John 3:15–18). In John 14:6 (NKJV), Jesus said, "I am the way, the truth, and the life. No one comes to the Father except through Me." Does the book or doctrine of your religion contradict the words of Jesus Himself?

Any teaching that denies the deity of Christ is false, according to the Word of God. There are numerous verses in the Bible that verify Jesus Christ is God.[51] Colossians 2:9 (NLT) says, "For in Christ lives all the fullness of God in a human body." In the New Testament, five writers testify to the deity of Christ, and Jesus referred to Himself as God (John 5:18). In Hebrews, God the Father says the Son is God. "But to the Son he says, 'Your throne, O God, endures forever and ever.'" (Hebrews 1:8 NLT). What is the stance of your religion on the deity of Christ?

Teachings that add human works to salvation go against what the Bible says. The thief that hung on a cross near Jesus and accepted Him as the Messiah was told, "And Jesus replied, 'I assure you, today you will be with me in paradise'" (Luke 23:43 NLT). The thief would be where Jesus was in paradise even though he had no "works" to substantiate his worthiness. When Jesus gave His last breath on the cross, He said, "It is finished!" (John 19:30 NLT) Jesus didn't say, "Now go and do works so you can make it to heaven." Why would He suffer a horrific death if we had to add to it with our meager human effort? Romans 11:6 (NLT) says, "And since it is through God's kindness, then it is not by their good works. For in that case, God's grace would not be what it really is—free and undeserved." Ephesians 2:9 (ESV) says, "not a result of works, so that no one may boast." Galatians 1:6–9 warns against turning to a different gospel and warns of a curse on those who teach it. What do the words you are following tell you?

Another test is on sin. The Bible says that in Christ, we are a new creation (2 Corinthians 5:17). Therefore, when we accept Jesus, we desire to change our worldly ways. A religion that teaches that the prayer of salvation gives license to live in sin is false. When we choose salvation, we receive the Holy Spirit and He indwells us. When we truly accept the Lord, we desire to please Him, and He cannot abide by sin. Matthew 7:21 (NLT) says, "Not everyone who calls out to me, 'Lord! Lord!' will enter the Kingdom of Heaven. Only those who actually do the will of my Father in heaven will enter." What is your religion teaching?

When people believe they need to "work" their way to heaven, there is always doubt in their minds. Have they done enough to reach the kingdom of God? Romans 8:14–17 tells us that we received the Spirit of God through adoption, and we do not have to live in fear. Because we are adopted through our belief in Christ, we are heirs to the kingdom of the Lord. This is through faith that what Jesus did on the cross is enough. Otherwise, what was the point of Jesus' death?

Are you living with the fear of not doing enough? Or do you know without a shadow of a doubt that you will go to heaven? There are also those living in sin who falsely believe they are right with the Lord. How can a sinful person be right with God when He can't tolerate sin? When we are genuinely saved, we desire to please the Lord, and to do that, we must reject sin in our lives. No one will ever be perfect, but we must pursue the Perfector of our faith (Hebrews 12:2).

When people apply the "good, better, best" logic to salvation, they play a dangerous game because some use that as a license to sin. Some people falsely believe they must work their way to heaven, but if they do not achieve perfection, they will still reside in paradise, and that is not accurate. The Bible does not speak of multiple layers of heaven for the believers' final residence. The Bible refers to three heavens, beginning with the heaven that gives rain, which is the atmosphere (James 5:18), the heaven where the sun and moon are darkened and the stars fall, which is outer space (Matthew 24:29 NLT), and the highest heaven—the home of God (1 Kings 8:27 NLT).[52] Hebrews 9:27 tells us that we have one life to live; we will die once, and after that is judgment. For human beings, perfection is impossible, so salvation can only be obtained through a belief in our Lord and Savior Jesus Christ. There are no second chances after we die.

Now, do you want the good news? As long as you are still breathing on this earth, there is hope. The Bible says we need to turn from our wicked ways and call out to God, and He will hear and forgive (2 Chronicles 7:14).

Second Corinthians 1:22 ensures the saved ones that God has placed His ownership upon us and placed His Spirit within us. All we have to do is believe that Jesus died on the cross for our sins, admit we are sinners, turn from sin, and accept the free gift of salvation. Isn't that fantastic news? Our home in heaven is not something to be achieved but received.

We live in an exciting time, and the revelation of Bible prophecy is playing out around us. Be happy and rejoice because the promise of heaven is near. Can you imagine a perfect place devoid of pain or sickness? The Bible tells us that every tear of those in heaven will be wiped away by God Himself (Revelation 21:4). Can you imagine a place more beautiful than anything here on earth? What a glorious promise!

We are not on this earth for personal gain or our pursuit of happiness. If we are in Christ, we are here for Him. God knows the day we will be born and the day we will pass away because it was determined before we walked this earth. Nothing is a surprise to the Lord, and the year 2020 did not catch Him off guard. He knew it was coming well in advance because He knows and controls all. When we worry, we pine over things out of our control. However, when we give it to God, we can sleep in peace. Romans 8:28 (NLT) says, "And we know that God causes everything to work together for the good of those who love God and are called according to his purpose for them."

We have many glorious promises from God. We should desire all would seek Him and abide in His love and forgiveness. If you are not living in the peace of God's promise, I pray you will change that today.

God is waiting. Matthew 7:7 (ESV) says, "Ask, and it will be given to you; seek, and you will find; knock, and the door will be opened to you."

Looking back over my life, I know I had plans for the days I walked this earth. I had my hopes and dreams based on my limited view, but God had a different plan. The Lord implements His will on infinite wisdom, and His vision has far exceeded my expectations.

Look up! Seek God's plan for your life because it is perfect.

"For I know the plans I have for you,"
says the Lord.
"They are plans for good
and not for disaster,
to give you a future and a hope."
Jeremiah 29:11 NLT

Bibliography

AP News. "'Principle' Suspect in Mexican Drug Slayings Arrested in Arizona With PM-Ritual Slayings," April 21, 1989, accessed July 28, 2020. https://apnews.com/60b5d94a935feebecdd7b913c0d24792.

Barnhart, Melissa. "Harvest America: All Roads Lead to God But Only One Road Leads to Heaven, Through Jesus Christ." *The Christian Post,* October 6, 2014. https://www.christianpost.com/news/harvest-america-there-are-many-roads-to-god-but-only-one-road-to-heaven-through-jesus-christ.html.

Bible Hub. 2004–2021. Accessed January 9, 2020. https://biblehub.com/.

Bible Study Tools. "Bible Story of Jezebel." December 13, 2018. https://www.biblestudytools.com/bible-stories/bible-story-of-jezebel.html.

Boquet, Fr. Shenan J. "The Late-Term Abortion Horror." *Human Life International,* February 4, 2019. Accessed September 10, 2020. https://www.hli.org/2019/02/the-late-term-abortion-horror/.

Cameron, Barry. "Don't Give Up On Your Dream." *Crossroads,* May 29, 2015. Accessed July 22, 2020. https://www.crossroadschristian.org/blogs/blog/27548548-dont-give-up-on-your-dream.

Canfield, Jack, Mark Victor Hansen, and Les Hewitt. *The Power of Focus.* Deerfield Beach: Health Communications Inc., 2000.

Charlotte Lozier Institute."New Study: Abortion after Prenatal Diagnosis of Down Syndrome Reduces Down Syndrome Community by Thirty Percent." April 1, 2015. Accessed September 1, 2020. https://lozier-institute.org/new-study-abortion-after-prenatal-diagnosis-of-down-syndrome-reduces-down-syndrome-community-by-thirty-percent/#_edn6.

Chute, Rev. Author C. *William Carey. A Sketch Of Beginnings in Modern Missions.* Chicago: Goodman & Dickerson. 1891. Accessed February 10, 2021. https://www.wmcarey.edu/carey/chute1/chute1.htm.

Cole, Nicolas. "15 Sad Reasons People Give Up On Their Dreams." *Inc.,* November 30, 2017. https://www.inc.com/nicolas-cole/15-sad-reasons-people-give-up-on-their-dreams.html.

Dangerousroads. "Siskiyou Summit, one of the more perilous sections of Interstate 5." Accessed June 21, 2020. https://www.dangerousroads.org/north-america/usa/3775-siskiyou-summit.html.

———"Tejon Pass, a steep paved road." Accessed June 20, 2020. https://www.dangerousroads.org/north-america/usa/4366-tejon-pass.html.

Deis, Robert. "'When it rains, it pours' started out as a good thing. . . " November 6, 2013. http://www.thisdayinquotes.com/2009/11/when-it-rains-it-pours-started-out-as_06.html.

Department of Homeland Security. ICE. "Human Smuggling Equals Grave Danger, Big Money." January 16, 2018. Accessed July 28, 2020. https://www.ice.gov/features/human-smuggling-danger.

Diego, U-T San. "Border Tunnels: Complete List of Those Found." *San Diego Union-Tribune,* October 31 2013. Accessed August 16, 2020. https://www.sandiegouniontribune.com/news/border-baja-california/sdut-border-tunnels-2013oct31-htmlstory.html.

Dolce, Michael. "We Have Set Up a System to Sex Traffic American Children." *Newsweek*, January 1, 2018. Accessed February 10, 2021. https://www.newsweek.com/we-have-set-system-sex-traffic-american-children-779541.

Donnell, Marisa. "36 Definitions Of Love, According to Urban Dictionary." April 4, 2016. Accessed July 8, 2020. https://thoughtcatalog.com/marisa-donnelly/2016/04/36-definitions-of-love-according-to-urban-dictionary/.

Glennon, John C. "Tejon Pass, aka The Grapevine." Accessed June 20, 2020. http://www.crashforensics.com/tejonpass.cfm.

Glover, Scott. "FBI makes a connection between long-haul truckers, serial killings." *Los Angeles Times*, April 5, 2009. https://www.latimes.com/archives/la-xpm-2009-apr-05-me-serialkillers5-story.html.

Got Questions. Your Questions. Biblical Answers. "What is false doctrine?" Accessed December 19, 2020. https://www.gotquestions.org/false-doctrine.html.

"Who were the authors of the books of the Bible?" Accessed December 22, 2020. https://www.gotquestions.org/Bible-authors.html.

Graham, Billy. "Answers." January 26, 2020. Accessed August 28, 2020. https://billygraham.org/answer/my-ex-boyfriend-talked-me-into-getting-an-abortion-i-know-god-wont-forgive-me/.

Green, Lisa Cannon. "Women Distrust Church on Abortion." November 23, 2015. Accessed September 2, 2020. https://lifewayresearch.com/2015/11/23/women-distrust-church-on-abortion/.

Hall, Delaney. "The Tunnel." January 29, 2019. Accessed July 28, 2020. https://99percentinvisible.org/episode/the-tunnel/.

Hewitt, Les and Dr. Charlie Self. "Seeking God, Finding Purpose," in *The Power of Faithful Focus.* Deerfield Beach: Health Communications Inc., 2004, 1–30.

History. "U.S. Army Liberates Dachau Concentration Camp." *Last Updated* April 27, 2020. Accessed July 15, 2020. https://www.history.com/this-day-in-history/dachau-liberated.

————"Benedict Arnold." *Last Updated* January 16, 2020. Accessed January 27, 2020. https://www.history.com/topics/american-revolution/benedict-arnold.

Hodson, Natalie. "What My 21 Day Challange Means to Me." June 13, 2019. Accessed February 10, 2021. https://nataliehodson.com/what-my-21-day-challenge-means-to-me/.

hrf. "*19 Shocking Post Abortion Depression Statistics.*" Accessed September 11, 2020. https://healthresearchfunding.org/19-shocking-post-abortion-depression-statistics/.

Ingram, Chip. "How God Can Heal Your Emotional Pain." *Living on the Edge.* Accessed June 28, 2020. https://livingontheedge.org/2018/04/17/how-god-can-heal-your-emotional-pain/.

J&M Tank Lines. "How Trucking Culture Has Changed And How It Has Stayed The Same Over The Years." August 6, 2019. https://www.jmtank.com/2019/08/06/how-trucking-culture-has-changed-and-how-it-has-stayed-the-same-over-the-years/.

Jenkins, Dave. "7 Valuable Ways to Know if Something Is God's Will." December 15, 2020. Accessed December 17, 2020. https://www.biblestudytools.com/bible-study/topical-studies/valuable-ways-to-know-if-something-is-gods-will.html?utm_source=today%27s+bible+break-out&utm_campaign=today%27s+topical+bible+study+-+biblestudytools.com&utm_medium=email&utm_content=4068173&bcid.

Jeremiah, Dr. David. "What It Means to Be Clay in the Hands of the Potter," *David Jeremiah (blog)* Accessed November 11, 2020. https://davidjeremiah.blog/what-it-means-to-be-clay-in-the-hands-of-the-potter/.

Kilinc, Attila. "What Causes a Volcano to Erupt, and How Do Scientists Predict Eruptions?" November 29, 1999. Accessed November 5, 2020. https://www.scientificamerican.com/article/what-causes-a-volcano-to-erupt-and-how-do-scientists-predict-eruptions/.

Kuja, Marie-Claire. "The impact of negative words on self-esteem." February 24, 2016. https://www.worldpulse.com/community/users/kuja-mac12/posts/64686.

Bibliography

kyPhrase: Learn About Phrases and Sayings. "The Straw That Broke The Camel's Back." Accessed July 8, 2020. https://knowyourphrase.com/the-straw-that-broke-camels-back.

Laurie, Greg. "Angels and Demons Part 1." August 29, 2019. Video, 47:24. https://www.youtube.com/watch?v=f5t-CSr9RXA.

————. "Angels and Demons Part 2." August 29, 2019. Video, 48:42. https://www.youtube.com/watch?v=oaALmEvRQ9k.

————. "Forgiveness is not Optional." May 18, 2019. https://harvest.org/resources/gregs-blog/post/forgiveness-is-not-optional/.

Les Brown Enterprises. "About Les Brown." Accessed October 3, 2020. https://lesbrown.com/about/.

Lewis, Tanya. "5 Facinating Facts About Fetal Ultrasound." May 16, 2013. Accessed August 28, 2020. https://www.livescience.com/32071-history-of-fetal-ultrasound.html.

McCoy, Katie. "What does the Bible say about sexual assault?" February 5, 2015. https://biblicalwoman.com/bible-sexual-assault-women/.

McCray, Michael. "Ten Thousand Talents (Matthew 18:21–35)." October 21, 2012. Accessed October 28, 2020. https://godsambassadors.com/2012/10/21/ten-thousand-talents/.

Meek, David. "How Hot Does It Get In Phoenix Arizona?" *The Arizona Report (blog)*. Phoenix: Keller Williams Arizona Realty, June 19, 2016. https://arizonareport.com/how-hot-does-it-get-in-phoenix/.

Meyer, Josh. "Drug cartels raise the stakes on human smuggling." March 23, 2009. Accessed July 29, 2020. https://www.latimes.com/archives/la-xpm-2009-mar-23-na-human-smuggling23-story.html.

National Geographic Resourse Library. "Controlled Burning." Accessed December 18, 2020. https://www.nationalgeographic.org/encyclopedia/controlled-burning/.

Newton, Melanie. "Lesson 2: God's Power, Presence, And Perception (the Omnis)." February 12, 2019. https://bible.org/seriespage/lesson-2-god-s-power-presence-and-perception-omnis.

Olohan, Mary Margaret. "This Is What Women Who Regret Their Abortions Want Other Women To Know." July 20, 2019. Accessed August 28, 2020. https://dailycaller.com/2019/07/20/women-abortion-stories-regret/.

Richard, Guy M. "Expect Great Things from God." *TABLETALK.* December 27, 2019. https://tabletalkmagazine.com/posts/expect-great-things-from-god-2019-12/.

Rose, Lila and Daniel Gade. "Disability-Based Abortion is Legal Discrimination." August 9, 2019. Accessed August 28, 2020. https://thehill.com/opinion/healthcare/456841-disability-based-abortion-is-lethal-discrimination.

Russell, Chris. "Don't Edit God's Words." *Bible Study Tools (blog)*, https://www.biblestudytools.com/blogs/chris-russell/don-t-edit-god-s-words.html

Smith, Joe. "Murphy's Law Origin." Accessed October 12, 2020. https://www.murphys-laws.com/murphy/murphy-true.html#:~:text=Murphy%27s%20laws%20origin.%20Murphy%27s%20Law%20%28%221f%20anything%20can,deceleration%20a%20person%20can%20stand%20in%20a%20crash.

Smith, Samuel. "70% Of Women Who Get Abortions Identify as Christian, Survey Finds." November 25, 2015. Accessed September 10, 2020. https://www.christianpost.com/news/70-of-women-who-get-abortions-identify-as-christians-survey-finds.html?page=1.

Stanley, Charles F. "We may not see the big picture of our life, but God does." August 19, 2016. https://www.intouch.org/read/magazine/the-pulpit/piece-by-piece.

Stewart, Don. "Evil Angels, Demons, And The Occult The Dark World." San Dimas, California: EOW (Educating Our World) 2020. Accessed August 3, 2020. https://educatingourworld.com/images/PDFs/Unseen-World/evil-angels-demons-the-occult.pdf.

———. "Heaven, The Final Destination Of Belivers." San Dimas, California: EOW (Educating Our World) 2020. http://www.educatingourworld.com/images/PDFs/The-Afterlife/heaven-the-final-destination-of-believers.pdf

————. "Satan Our Advisary The Devil." (San Dimas, California: EOW (Educating Our World) 2020). Accessed August 22, 2020. http://www.educatingourworld.com/images/PDFs/Unseen-World/satan.pdf.

————. "Ten Reasons To Trust The Bible (Formerly titled The Ten Wonders Of The Bible)." San Dimas, California: EOW (Educating Our World) 2020. http://www.educatingourworld.com/images/PDFs/Bible/ten-reasons-to-trust-the-bible.pdf.

————. "What Everyone Needs To Know About Jesus." (San Dimas, California: EOW (Educating Our World) 2020). http://www.educatingourworld.com/images/PDFs/Jesus/what-everyone-needs-to-know-about-jesus.pdf.

Sweet, Rose. "Forgiveness and Restoration." January 1, 2001. https://www.focusonthefamily.com/marriage/forgiveness-and-restoration/.

Trevizo, Paul. "Ministering in Brutal Altar, Mexico." January 30, 2019. Accessed July 29, 2020. https://tucson.com/news/local/border/ministering-in-brutal-altar-mexico/article_aacee843-0c7a-5b0a-bbce-3afbfe8c-8ba4.html.

Vaca, Monica. "The top frauds of 2019." January 23, 2020. https://www.consumer.ftc.gov/blog/2020/01/top-frauds-2019.

Verret, Bethany. "Stop Misusing Jeremiah 29:11 and Understand the Real Meaning of 'For I Know the Plans I Have for You'." May 26, 2020. Accessed December 17, 2020. https://www.biblestudytools.com/bible-study/topical-studies/valuable-ways-to-know-if-something-is-gods-will.html?utm_source=today%27s+bible+breakout&utm_campaign=today%27s+topical+bible+study+-+biblestudytools.com&utm_medium=email&utm_content=4068173&bcid.

Wagner, Dennis. "Border Ranchers in a World Without a Wall." *USA Today*, 2017. Accessed July 29, 2020. https://www.usatoday.com/border-wall/story/us-ranchers-deal-with-migrants-border-crossers-mexico/559702001/.

Warrell, Margie. "See The Glass Half Full Or Empty? Why Optimists Are Happier, Healthier & Wealthier." *Forbes,* September 19, 2012. Accessed July 14, 2020. https://www.forbes.com/sites/margiewarrell/2012/09/19/see-the-glass-half-empty-or-full-7-keys-for-optimism-in-tough-times/#76ea196a767f.

Webster Dictionary, s.v. n.d. "*godliness.*" Accessed February 10, 2021. https://www.webster-dictionary.org/definition/Godliness.

Wikipedia. "Trucking industry in popular culture (United States)." Accessed June 10, 2020. https://en.wikipedia.org/wiki/Trucking_industry_in_popular_culture_(United_States).

About the Author

Tracey Glenn is a born-again child of God and a Jesus freak. She is a writer, blogger, and searcher of biblical wisdom. With a heart for God, kids, and all God's creatures, Tracey shares her journey through the pages of her life as a seeker of the Lord. She is a graduate of the School of Hard Knocks, and the Lord has used that education to transform her into a new creation. Tracey has an associate degree in psychology, has completed the Living Waters School of Biblical Evangelism, and is a successful entrepreneur.

Raised on a cattle ranch in southeast Arizona, Tracey has been married for over thirty years to the love of her life, Link, and she is a mother of three and grandmother of four. She has raised a child with special needs and is currently homeschooling. She cofounded a business in 2007, which at present has six locations across southern Arizona and provides other special needs children and their families with essential support and services. Involvement in helping others in need ultimately led her and her husband to adopt their son in 2013. You can learn more about Tracey and subscribe to her Branded In Faith blog on her website www.brandedinfaith.com, or connect with her on Facebook @brandedinfaith or Instagram @brandedinfaith. *Gathering the Wayward Heart* is Tracey's first book of, God-willing, many more to come.

Endnotes

Chapter 1

1 Kuja, "*The impact of negative.*"

2 Donnell, "*36 Definitions Of Love.*"

3 McCoy, "*What does the Bible.*"

Chapter 2

4 Wikipedia, "*Trucking industry in popular.*"; J&M Tank Lines, "*How Trucking Culture Has.*"

5 Glover, "*Trucker, Serial Killers.*"; Wikipedia, "*Trucking industry in popular.*"

6 Laurie, "*Angels and Demons Part 1.*"; Laurie, "*Angels and Demons Part 2.*"

7 Dangerous Roads, "A Steep Paved Road"; Glennon, "*Tejon Pass.*"

Chapter 3

8 Meek, "How Hot In Phoenix."

9 Dangerous Roads, "*Siskiyou Summit.*"

10 Laurie, "*Angels and Demons Part 1.*"; Laurie, "*Angels and Demons Part 2.*"

Chapter 4

11 Newton, "Power, Presence, And Perception"; Stanley, "Big Picture of Life."

12 Cole, "Reasons People Give Up."

13 Cameron, "Don't Give Up."

14 Staff, *Bible Story of Jezebel.*

15 Deis, *When it rains.*

16 Vaca, *top frauds of 2019.*

17 Warrell, *Why Optimists Are Happier.*

18 Les Brown Enterprises, "About Les Brown."

19 Richard, "Great Things From God"; Chute, "William Carey," 24–25.

Chapter 5

20 APNews, *Mexican Drug Slayings*

21 Diego, *Border Tunnels*; Hall, *The Tunnel.*

22 ICE, *Human Smuggling*; Meyer, *stakes on human smuggling.*

23 Wagner, *World Without a Wall.*

24 Stewart, *Evil Angels, Demons*; Stewart, *Satan Our Advisary.*

25 Meyer, *stakes on human smuggling.*

Chapter 6

26 Boquet, *Late-Term Abortion Horror.*

27 Rose and Gade, "Disability-Based Abortion."

28 Charlotte Lozier Institute, "Abortion After Prenatal Diagnosis."

29 Olohan, "Women Who Regret Abortion"; Wehrli, *Women Who Regretted Abortion.*

30 Olohan, *Women Who Regret Abortion.*

31 Green, *Women Distrust Church.*

32 Smith, "Women Who Get Abortions"; Green, "Distrust Church on Abortion."

33 Graham, *Answers.*

Chapter 7

34 Smith, "*Murphy's Law Origin.*"

Chapter 8

35 Laurie, "Forgiveness is not Optional"; Sweet, "Forgiveness And Restoration."

36 Laurie, "Forgiveness is not Optional"; Sweet, "Forgiveness And Restoration."

37 Kilinc, "*What Causes a Volcano.*"

38 McCray, "Ten Thousand Talents."

39 History.com, "*U.S. Army Liberates Dachau.*"

Chapter 9

40 Hewitt, and Self, "The Power of Faithful Focus," 1–30.

Chapter 10

41 Webster, "godliness."

Chapter 11

42 Dolce, "*Sex Traffic American Children.*"

43 National Geographic, "Controlled Burning."

44 Verret, "Understand The Real Meaning."

45 Hodson, "My 21 Day Challenge."

Conclusion

46 Got Questions, "*What is false doctrine.*"

47 Barnhart, "*All Roads Lead.*"

48 Stewart, "Trust the Bible," 15–17.

49 Russell, "Don't Edit God's Words."

50 Got Questions, "*What is false doctrine.*"

51 Stewart, "Know About Jesus," 42–50.

52 Stewart, "Final Destination of believers," 43–48.

Order Information

CPSIA information can be obtained
at www.ICGtesting.com
Printed in the USA
JSHW021214280122
22352JS00003B/16